CYBERSAFETY

Identity Theft

CYBERSAFETY

CYBERSAFETY

Identity Theft

JOHN VACCA

MARY E. VACCA

CONSULTING EDITOR

MARCUS K. ROGERS, Ph.D., CISSP, DFCP

**Founder and Director,
Cyber Forensics Program,
Purdue University**

CHELSEA HOUSE
An Infobase Learning Company

Cybersafety: Identity Theft

Copyright © 2012 by Infobase Learning

Chelsea House
An Infobase Learning Company
132 West 31st Street
New York NY 10001

Library of Congress Cataloging-in-Publication Data
Vacca, John R.
  Identity theft / John Vacca ; Marcus K. Rogers, consulting editor. — 1st ed.
     p. cm. — (Cybersafety)
  Includes bibliographical references and index.
  ISBN-13: 978-1-60413-700-2 (hardcover : alk. paper)
  ISBN-10: 1-60413-700-2 (hardcover : alk. paper) 1. Identity theft—Juvenile literature. 2. Identity theft—Prevention. I. Title. II. Series.
  HV6675.V293 2011
  332.024—dc22

                    2011005643

Chelsea House books are available at special discounts when purchased in bulk quantities for businesses, associations, institutions, or sales promotions. Please call our Special Sales Department in New York at (212) 967-8800 or (800) 322-8755.

You can find Chelsea House on the World Wide Web at http://www.infobasepublishing.com

Text design by Erik Lindstrom
Composition by EJB Publishing Services
Cover design by Takeshi Takahashi
Cover printed by Yurchak Printing, Landisville, Pa.
Book printed and bound by Yurchak Printing, Landisville, Pa..
Date printed: March 2012

Printed in the United States of America

This book is printed on acid-free paper.

CONTENTS

Foreword

The Internet has had and will continue to have a profound effect on society. It is hard to imagine life without such technologies as computers, cell phones, gaming devices, and so on. The Internet, World Wide Web, and their associated technologies have altered our social and personal experience of the world. In no other time in history have we had such access to knowledge and raw information. One can search the Library of Congress, the Louvre in Paris, and read online books and articles or watch videos from just about any country in the world. We can interact and chat with friends down the street, in another state, or halfway around the globe. The world is now our neighborhood. We are a "wired" society that lives a significant amount of our life online and tethered to technology.

The Internet, or cyberspace, is a great enabler. What is also becoming apparent, though, is that there is a dark side to this global wired society. As the concept of who our friends are moves from real world relationships to cyberspace connections, so also do the rules change regarding social conventions and norms. How many friends do we have online that we have actually met in person? Are online-only friends even real or at the very least whom they claim to be? We also begin to redefine privacy. Questions arise over what should be considered private or public information. Do we really want every-one in the global society to have access to our personal information? As with the real world there may be people online that we do not wish to associate with or grant access to our lives.

It is easy to become enamored with technology and the technol-ogy/information revolution. It is equally as easy to become paranoid about the dangers inherent in cyberspace. What is difficult but neces-sary is to be realistic about how our world has been forever changed. We see numerous magazine, TV, and newspaper headlines regarding the latest cybercrime attacks. Stories about identity theft being the fastest growing nonviolent criminal activity are common. The govern-ment is concerned with cyber or information warfare attacks against critical infrastructures. Given this kind of media coverage it is easy to think that the sky is falling and cyberspace is somehow evil. Yet if we step back and think about it, technology is neither good nor bad, it simply *is*. Technology is neutral; it is what we do with technology that determines whether it improves our lives or damages and makes our lives more difficult. Even if someone is on the proverbial fence over whether the Internet and cyberspace are society enablers or disablers, what is certain is that the technology genie is out of the bottle. We will never be able to put it back in; we need to learn how to master and live with it.

Learning to live with the Internet and its technological offshoots is one of the objectives behind the Cybersafety series of books. The immortal words of Sir Francis Bacon (the father of the scientific method), "knowledge is power," ring especially true today. If we live in a society that is dependent on technology and therefore we live a significant portion of our daily lives in cyberspace, then we need to understand the potential downside as well as the upside. However, what is not useful is fear mongering or the demonization of technology.

There is no doubt that cyberspace has its share of bad actors and criminals. This should not come as a surprise to anyone. Cyberspace mirrors traditional society, including both the good and unfortunately the bad. Historically criminals have been attracted to new technologies in an effort to improve and extend their criminal methods. The same advantages that technology and cyberspace bring to our normal everyday lives (e.g., increased communication, the ability to remotely access information) can be used in a criminal manner. Online fraud, identity theft, cyberstalking, and cyberbullying are but a few of the ugly behaviors that we see online today.

Navigating successfully through cyberspace also means that we need to understand how the "cyber" affects our personality and social behavior. One of the empowering facets of cyberspace and technology is the fact that we can escape reality and find creative outlets for ourselves. We can immerse ourselves in computer and online games, and if so inclined, satisfy our desire to gamble or engage in other risky behaviors. The sense of anonymity and the ability to redefine who we are online can be intoxicating to some people. We can experiment with new roles and behaviors that may be polar opposites of who we are in the real physical world. Yet, as in the real world, our activities and behaviors in cyberspace have consequences too. Well-meaning escapism can turn to online addictions; seemingly harmless distractions like online gaming can consume so much of our time that our real world relationships and lives are negatively affected. The presumed anonymity afforded by cyberspace can lead to bullying and stalking, behaviors that can have a profound and damaging impact on the victims and on ourselves.

The philosophy behind the Cybersafety series is based on the recognition that cyberspace and technology will continue to play an increasingly important part of our everyday lives. The way in which we define who we are, our home life, school, social relationships, and work life will all be influenced and impacted by our online behaviors and misbehaviors. Our historical notions of privacy will also be redefined in terms of universal access to our everyday activities and posted musings. The Cybersafety series was created to assist us in understanding and making sense of the online world. The intended audience for the series is those individuals who are and will be the most directly affected by cyberspace and its technologies, namely young people (i.e., those in grades 6–12).

Young people are the future of our society. It is they who will go forward and shape societal norms, customs, public policy, draft new laws, and be our leaders. They will be tasked with developing positive coping mechanisms for both the physical and cyberworlds. They will have dual citizenship responsibilities: citizens of the physical and of the cyber. It is hoped that this series will assist in providing insight, guidance, and positive advice for this journey.

The series is divided into books that logically gather related concepts and issues. The goal of each book in the series is not to scare but to educate and inform the reader. As the title of the series states the focus is on "safety." Each book in the series provides advice on what to watch out for and how to be safer. The emphasis is on education and awareness while providing a frank discussion related to the consequences of certain online behaviors.

It is my sincere pleasure and honor to be associated with this series. As a former law enforcement officer and current educator, I am all too aware of the dangers that can befall our young people. I am also keenly aware that young people are more astute than some adults commonly give them credit for being. Therefore it is imperative that we begin a dialogue that enhances our awareness and encourages and challenges the reader to reexamine their behaviors and attitudes toward cyberspace and technology. We fear what we do not understand; fear is not productive, but knowledge is empowering. So let's begin our collective journey into arming ourselves with more knowledge.

—Marcus K. Rogers, Ph.D., CISSP, DFCP,

Founder and Director,

Cyber Forensics Program,

Purdue University

Acknowledgments

There are many people whose efforts on this book have contributed to its successful completion. I owe each a debt of gratitude and want to take this opportunity to offer my sincere thanks. A very special thanks to my editor and publisher James Chambers, without whose continued interest and support this book would not have been possible. And, thanks to editorial assistant Matt Anderson, who provided staunch support and encouragement when it was most needed. Thanks to my copyeditor, Pamela Fehl, whose fine editorial work has been invaluable. And, a special thanks to consulting editor Marc Rogers, who wrote the foreword for this book. Also, thanks to all of the other people at Chelsea House Publishing whose many talents and skills are essential to a finished book. Finally, thanks to my wife, Bee Vacca, for her love, her help, and her understanding of my long work hours.

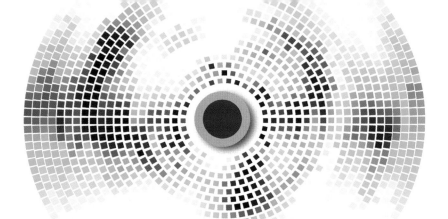

Introduction:
An Overview
of Identity Theft

Identity theft happens when someone uses an individual's personal and financial information to perpetuate fraud and a host of other crimes. While it is not something new in the world, today's technological society has made it easier for people to steal a person's legal and financial identity (names, Social Security numbers, credit and debit cards, and so on), and wreak havoc with it. Identity thieves may steal a person's credit card information and pile as many charges as the credit limit will allow. The thieves may take out a new credit card in a person's name and have the bill sent to their own address. Perhaps they will get a telephone in their victim's name and run up a bill. In at least one case a person's identity was stolen and the thief actually improved the person's credit score! The salient point here is that with identification numbers, an identity thief functions as another person, be it for good or ill. The damage to a person's credit history could go on indefinitely, or until that person is contacted by someone trying to collect a debt. According to the Federal Trade

Commission (FTC), "As many as 13 million Americans have their identities stolen each year; and, that number is rapidly increasing each year."[1]

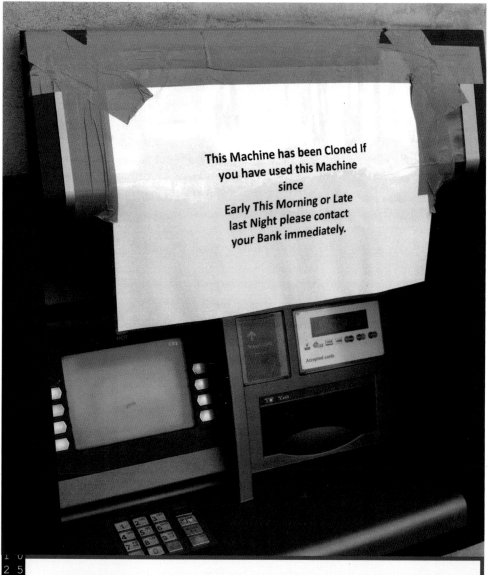

Criminals taking advantage of modern technology have developed methods to steal private financial information. People who use Internet banking, e-mail, and ATMs are vulnerable to identity theft. *(Source: Tom Stoddart/Getty Images)*

THE HOWS OF STEALING AN IDENTITY

Today the stealing of personal information is as good as it gets for criminals. It is easy money. There are many ways, off-line and online, that professional identity thieves obtain an individual's legal, private, personal, and financial information. These include the following:

- **Change of Address:** This is the completion of a change of address form to divert the billing statements of the victim to the thief's location. The identity thieves may actually call a lender and request a change of address over the phone.
- **Dumpster Diving:** Basically, it is the art of going through someone's trash to find personal identification clues. Trash is a great source of information!
- **Pretexting:** Sometimes identity thieves get enough information about a victim from another source, which allows them to impersonate the victim with a utility company or a financial institution. The thieves use a false pretext to access an account to get more personal information.
- **Pharming:** In this scam, the perpetrators hijack a legitimate Web site and redirect that site's users to an illicit Web site, which they hope will trick users into divulging personal data or account information.
- **Phishing:** This is a type of deception designed to steal a person's valuable personal data, such as e-mail account information, credit card numbers, or other account data and passwords. The thief contacts the victim via e-mail, pretending to be a bank or other legitimate company, and requests that the victim provide data about the account.
- **Skimming:** People can purchase special technology that records credit card numbers when they are being swiped or as they are being entered. Collecting information by this method is called "skimming."
- **Stealing Data from Fax Machines:** Orders delivered by fax may include personal data and credit card information.

It is not uncommon for faxes to sit in the fax machine delivery tray in an office for some time before they are collected, where anyone—a delivery person, a visitor, a janitor, or a dishonest employee—can take them or steal the data they contain.

- **Telephone Services:** Identity thieves may use a victim's publicly available phone number to set up automated calling attempts, pretending to be conducting a survey or representing a bank, that request personal information.
- **Traditional Stealing:** The stealing of wallets and purses; mail, bank, and credit card statements; pre-approved credit offers; and new checks or tax information also gives identity thieves what they want. This usually involves the stealing of personnel information by bribing employees at targeted companies to divulge the information to which they have access.[2]
- **Hacking:** Identity thieves sometimes bypass computer security measures to illegally enter a company's or organization's computers, where they can steal personal information about that group's clients, customers, or members.

WHAT CRIMINALS DO WITH STOLEN IDENTITIES

There are many things a thief can do with a person's information once they have stolen it. They can use it to commit

- credit card fraud
- phone or utilities fraud
- bank/finance fraud
- government documents fraud[3]
- other types of fraud

Credit Card Fraud

According to the FTC, opening a new credit account in someone else's name is one way an identity thief may take advantage of having

SKIMMING

According to Jim and Audri Lanford of Internet ScamBusters (a scam resource center Web site), skimming is the process of secretly reading data off credit and debit cards. They estimate that skimming is cheating people in the United States out of as much as $4 billion a year. For instance, if a card gets skimmed the bank will probably refund the full amount of loss, provided that there is recorded documentation of the incident and the contract between the issuer and the victim states that the victim will be refunded if he or she incurs a loss. However, a person could spend years trying to sort out additional damage, especially if specific bank card details have been compromised and used by thieves to commit identity theft. All it takes for an identity thief to get access to bank and credit card numbers and their associated personal identification number (PIN) numbers is a little technology.

Installing cameras to record transactions at ATMs is one common way to skim information. Thieves use cameras to record the keys their victims press when they enter this PIN number. Videos available online show how easy it is. One example is here: http://www.youtube.com/watch?v=AY_SPP1loFs&NR=1. According to Internet ScamBusters, this video was posted by the European ATM Security Team (EAST) after it was confiscated from identity thieves. Because the spy camera the thieves installed was working when they set it up, the identity thieves accidentally recorded themselves hijacking an ATM. To see more examples of how skimmers work, check out the following video report exposing these scams in the United Kingdom: http://www.youtube.com/watch?v=63heiTqM4pg&feature=related.[4]

a person's identifying information. Identity thieves will mount up the charges, leaving a delinquent account that will find its way onto a person's credit report.[5]

Phone or Utilities Fraud

An identity thief who does not want to pay telephone charges for their home phone or cell may use someone else's identifying information to open up new accounts or to run up charges on an existing account. Also, an identity thief may have their utility services (like electricity, heating, or satellite television) turned on in someone else's name if they have the right personal data.[6]

Bank/Finance Fraud

Ordering new checks on another person's bank account can be a snap for an identity thief who has that person's account number and mailing address. In some cases of stolen identity, the thief

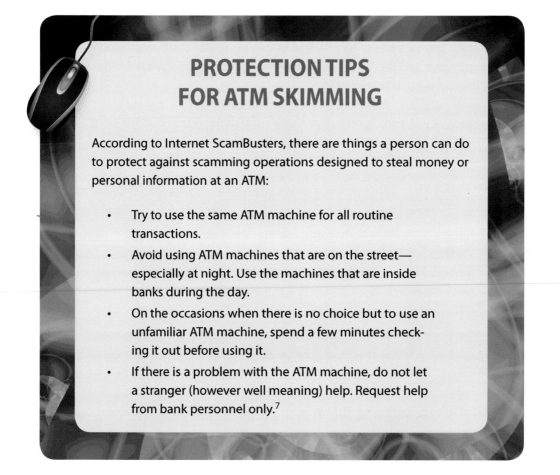

PROTECTION TIPS FOR ATM SKIMMING

According to Internet ScamBusters, there are things a person can do to protect against scamming operations designed to steal money or personal information at an ATM:

- Try to use the same ATM machine for all routine transactions.
- Avoid using ATM machines that are on the street—especially at night. Use the machines that are inside banks during the day.
- On the occasions when there is no choice but to use an unfamiliar ATM machine, spend a few minutes checking it out before using it.
- If there is a problem with the ATM machine, do not let a stranger (however well meaning) help. Request help from bank personnel only.[7]

might even open a new bank account in the person's name and write bad checks on the new account, leaving the innocent victim to take the fall.[8]

Government Documents Fraud

What about obtaining a new driver's license card with someone else's name? An identity thief could walk into a license bureau and say he has lost his license. He gives his victim's personal identification and has his picture taken and placed on the new license.[9]

Other Types of Fraud

Getting a new job in someone else's name means an enterprising identity thief gets the pay check while the victim pays the taxes. A person's personal health insurance information could give an identity thief access to medical services. Even renting a house in someone else's name is easy enough for an identity thief with the right credentials.[10]

HOW TO FIND IF AN IDENTITY WAS STOLEN

The best thing to do to protect against identity theft is to protect personal information. If potential identity thieves cannot get the information, they cannot use it. The next best thing a person can do is to stop identity theft before damages can mount up too heavily. How to do this:

- Monitor accounts regularly to be sure there are no unexpected transactions.
- Examine bank statements carefully to be sure there is no spurious activity that might have been performed by an identity thief.
- Keep a watchful eye on credit reports for any clues that there is a shadow personality sharing the report.[11]

The sad fact is that it is not possible to know that an identity has been stolen until some use of it has been made. Aside from regularly watching out for suspicious activity on accounts, there are less pleasant ways to find out that an identity has been stolen:

- Bill collection agencies may contact a person, demanding payment on a debt that the person never incurred.
- When a person applies for a car loan or mortgage, it might come to light that a problem with their credit history is preventing approval of the loan.
- An item in the mail referencing something that has (seemingly) nothing to do with that person (such as a job that a person does not have or a house they never bought), would be a clue that that person has been victimized by an identity thief.[12]

SPECIFIC STEPS THAT MUST BE TAKEN IF AN IDENTITY IS STOLEN

When a person has been a victim of identity theft, it is because some kind of crime against them has been committed. Whether the crime was a physical theft of identifying records (in a wallet or purse, for example) or whether another type of identity theft occurred that resulted in fraud of some kind, there are specific steps that must be taken immediately after learning that there has been a crime:

- file an Identity Theft Complaint with the FTC
- file a police report
- check credit reports
- notify creditors
- dispute any unauthorized transactions[13]

File an Identity Theft Complaint with the FTC

A form can be accessed online in order to file an ID Theft Complaint. Filling out this report is one step victims can take to protect themselves from consequences of the actions of identity theft.[16]

File a Police Report

An incident of identity theft should be filed with the local police. A copy of the Identity Theft Complaint that was filed with the FTC should also be made available to the officer taking the complaint.

First, in order to gain access to records of transactions entered into by the thief, a victim must have filed a specific and detailed Identity Theft Report. Records such as a thief's fraudulent application may be extremely useful in legally proving that a victim is, indeed, a victim.

Second, a victim may submit a copy of the Identity Theft Report to the three major credit reporting agencies (or to companies where the thief misused the information) in order to gain certain legal rights to which she is entitled. The three major agencies are Equifax, Experian, and TransUnion. Once the victim has received this report, these agencies must not use on her credit report any of the fraudulent information (like accounts or addresses) that came about as a result of the identity theft.

Finally, when presented with an Identity Theft Report, a company that has been cheated by an identity thief cannot try to collect a fraudulent debt from a victim of identity theft (or sell it to others for collection).[14]

Check Credit Reports

Once a person's identity has been stolen, the time and effort required to clear up the problems depends on the factors involved in the situation. What kind of theft was it? Did the thief sell the victim's information to other criminals? If the thief was caught, perhaps the problem is easier to set to rights. Have the credit reports been corrected?

Notify Creditors

Letting a company know immediately when there has been exposure of financial data, for example, if a purse or wallet was stolen or lost, is imperative. If fraudulent activity is detected on an account, contact the business immediately to report the problem.[15]

Dispute Any Unauthorized Transactions

Any unauthorized transaction that shows up on a bank statement or a credit card statement and any odd item appearing on bills from utilities or service providers warrants close scrutiny. It should be disputed with the company immediately.

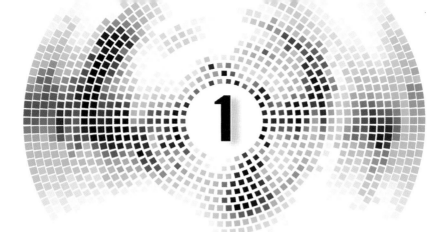

Identity Theft Defined

Seventeen-year-old Doyle Lamont was excited about buying his first car during his senior year in high school. The car dealership in Topeka, Kansas, where he was buying his vehicle, pulled up his credit report by using his Social Security number (SSN). Even though Doyle was young and had not yet built up a credit history, the salesman was shocked to find that another person (named Robert Trent) living in Syracuse, New York, had the same Social Security number as Doyle. In fact, that person had built up a credit score number of 816.

Doyle's father, who was cosigning for the car, asked the salesman for the address and phone number of Robert Trent. The salesman complied. Doyle and his father then left the dealership to file a report of the incident with the Topeka police department, place a call to the U.S. Social Security Administration Fraud Hotline at (800) 269-0271, and fill out the Fraud Reporting Form on the Social Security Administration's Web site.

In the meantime, Doyle's father called the car dealership back to get additional information about the incident. The dealership sales manager answered the phone and told Doyle's father that a clerical error was made in accessing his son's Social Security number earlier; therefore, the incident never happened. Furthermore, the manager told him that car salesmen are not allowed to give out contact information on another person. Doyle's father was shocked by the dealership's backpedaling on the incident.

A few months later, the Social Security Administration (SSA) contacted Doyle's father, and told him that his son's Social Security number had indeed been traced to a Robert Trent in Syracuse, New York. Robert Trent (alias Roberto Sanchez, Peter Cruise, Rick Monz, etc.) had just been arrested by the combined efforts of the Bureau of Alcohol, Tobacco, Firearms and Explosives (ATF) and the Drug Enforcement Administration (DEA) for trafficking drugs and firearms with the drug cartels in northern Mexico.

Doyle's father immediately had his son apply in person at the local SSA office to get a new number. The SSA helped Doyle complete a statement explaining why he needed a new number and the application for a new number. Today Doyle feels that it was a definite advantage to get rid of the old SSN, because he was not losing anything personal to him; he had not yet begun to build his credit. The whole ordeal lasted about three years, and he does not know to this day how Robert Trent got his information, nor how his old Social Security number is now in the hands of hundreds of illegal aliens.

Today incidents like Doyle Lamont's are occurring at an alarming rate. Social Security numbers are very important to individuals because they are unique legal links between an individual and his or her financial records throughout their past and into their future. A Social Security number is used to pay taxes, track a credit history, and access benefits and services. Many routine business and financial activities in which people participate, be it a job, bank loan, medical service, or any number of other activities, creates a legal record that documents the person's participation. That record is linked to the individual participant's Social Security number. In short, a Social Security number is the key to a person's business, financial, and legal history.[1]

IDENTITY THEFT HISTORY

The number and types of transactions an average person might perform on any given day are many. One person might rent a car or charge tickets to a ball game. Another might call home on a cell phone or apply for a credit card. Someone else might write a check to pay for groceries. These transactions, and many more like them, are part of everyday life, and few people think twice about them as they go through their day—except, that is, the individual who wants access to the information that might be disclosed in any given transaction. According to the FTC, "There were so many incidents of identity theft in the 1990s, that the Federal Trade Commission (FTC) began collecting information about this type of crime." Every complaint of an occurrence of identity theft was recorded in the FTC's national database known as the Identity Theft Data Clearinghouse. The FTC provides more information about this online at http://www.ftc.gov/bcp/edu/pubs/consumer/general/gen09.pdf. From then on, there has been a yearly increase in the number of complaints reported by victims, and "the FTC estimates that in 2010, the number of identity theft complaints recorded in the Clearinghouse from victims around the country numbered 800,000."

According to the FTC, "The data collected from a survey in 2009 showed that in the year prior to the survey, 3.2 million people had discovered that an identity thief had opened new accounts in their names. Another 6.6 million reported that they had been victims of some type of misuse of an existing account. Bottom line? More than 100 million people were victims of some form of identity theft during that period. Translate these reports to the corresponding financial repercussions and that equates to a $480 billion loss to business. Individual victims incurred nearly $50 billion in losses. Translate these reports to time required by victims and their families to resolve their problems and you get 3 billion hours." Not a pretty picture.[2]

Javelin Strategy & Research (a financial services, payments, mobile, and security research company) reported that "2010 saw the number of new accounts opened by identity thieves with their stolen information increase to 40 percent of all identity fraud crimes. This is a significant rise (up 6 percent) in this type of crime, as it only accounted for 34 percent of identity fraud crimes in 2009. There were nearly double the fraudulently opened new online accounts from the previous year. The number of new e-mail payment accounts also increased by 13 percent. A 2011 survey asked for the first time about mobile phone accounts opened fraudulently, and a surprising 30 percent of identity theft victims reported positively."[3]

No one is safe. Data shows that there is no primary target for identity theft in regards to race, age, gender, education levels, or existing wealth when it comes to the crimes of an identity thief. There are, in fact, some groups that are more likely to be victims. Children, young people in general, are at a higher risk. People who live in some parts of the country might be more vulnerable than people in others. However, there are 280 million credit files on people in the United States. And since identity theft appears to be an equal opportunity offender, there are 280 million people who are potential targets for an identity thief.

IDENTITY THEFT DEFINED

When someone uses another person's identifying information without permission as a means to gain goods and services, they have committed identity theft. A very common form of identity theft involves the use of a person's identifying information to open a new credit card account in the victim's name. How does an identity thief gain access to someone's identifying information? A person's everyday transactions make him or her vulnerable. Almost every financial transaction involves the sharing of some form of identifying information. It could be a person's name and address together with a bank card number or a telephone number. Some transactions require a Social Security number, such as when filling out personnel forms for a new job. An identity thief swipes a bit of personal information from someone, uses it to get some additional information, and parlays that information into a new identity. Is it possible to prevent identity theft from happening? The sad fact is that if someone is dead set on committing a crime involving identity, there is little an unsuspecting victim can do to prevent it. That is not to say that a person cannot make the effort to minimize the risk. They can certainly make it more difficult for a would-be thief to gain identifying information, so that a casual attempt at identity theft will be foiled. The key to such self-protection is the wise management of personal information and heightened sensitivity to the risks in everyday affairs. Sadly, it is those least likely to be accumulating credit records or monitoring their credit reports who are at a high risk: children and teens.

CHILD IDENTITY THEFT DEFINED

According to Javelin Strategy & Research, "Children who are between 11 and 18 years old and have their identifying data stolen by an identity thief fall into the category of Child Identity Theft." This group involves children in the sixth through the twelfth grades. Child identity theft means that a minor's personal identifying information is stolen and used in a fraudulent manner in order to achieve personal gain.[4]

Identity Stealing by Parents

Children are vulnerable to identity theft, and very often they are victimized by a close family friend, relative, or even their parents. ABC News reported on the following case of child identity theft by parents.

In 1998, Randy Waldron Jr. was 17 years old. He wanted to be an airline pilot and applied to every college that had a relevant program. Randy was rejected by every school he applied to. Why he was turned down was a mystery, because he had good grades in school. Randy began to receive rejection letters in response to his applications for financial aid and credit cards. Puzzled by what was happening to him, Randy finally wrote to get his free credit report. He was shocked by what he found. Randy's credit report was 50 pages long.

It seemed that Randy was $3.6 million in debt, and a convicted felon to boot! Upon investigation, he learned that he owed hundreds of thousands of dollars to MasterCard and Visa, and he owed back taxes to the state of Florida. Randy had liens filed against him as well as civil actions. A high school junior living in New Hampshire, he discovered that his father had stolen his Social Security number when he was only one year old.

When Randy was an infant, Waldron Sr. left Randy's mother and moved to Florida. By 1982, Waldron Sr., who was a charismatic, attractive, and seemingly successful man, had stolen his infant son's spotless identity and was using it as his own. His life, from that point on, became Randy Jr.'s problem.

Randy was one child out of thousands who become victims of child identity theft each year. These children are easy prey to any family member or family friend with money troubles. Their Social Security numbers can be had by people who work in the school systems or in hospitals and doctors' offices where it is relatively easy to gain access to the information. Social Security numbers are even sold illegally on the Internet. Children are particularly vulnerable because they have what the thief wants: a clean, untroubled credit history and background. Because Social Security numbers are not linked to their owners' names and ages, it is a simple thing for an identity thief to begin to use it as his own once he has it.

Randy's case was a particularly tragic one. It is very difficult to clear a person's name after having been saddled with such an unsavory history. Getting a new and untarnished Social Security number is difficult and takes time. It can also create new problems for a victim. It took nine years for Randy to get a new Social Security number. In the meanwhile, Randy was vulnerable to repercussions from his father's crimes. Randy found a job working as a flight attendant. In 2001, after the September 11 attacks, a background check found felony convictions on Randy's record (a gift from a "loving" parent) and he nearly lost his job.

For years, police (in two states) told Randy there was nothing they could do. The same story held true with the Social Security Administration. Luckily for Randy, by 2004, the problem with identity theft had become so prevalent that general comprehension of the problem and the associated laws regarding identity theft began to change things. Randy was finally issued a new identity. But that only unleashed a whole new host of problems. Because his identity had no history, the military threatened to arrest Randy for not having registered with the Selective Service System. He had no record of a driving history, so he found it difficult to get insurance. His young life history was lost in the switch to a new Social Security card, and thus Randy had no good history of his own to support him.[5]

HOW IDENTITY THEFT IS DONE

No matter how carefully people work to manage how their personal identifying information flows through the system, and no matter

AGE VERIFICATION

According to the Identity Theft Resource Center, "Most people think that credit issuers will know that an application is bogus because of the age of a victim." In fact, these companies, organizations, and agencies have no way to determine a potential customer's age based on identifying information. When an application is presented to a company, the age on the application is ordinarily presumed to be correct by the people who process the application. They do not often think to demand proof by asking to see a driver's license or other documentation.[6]

how hard they try to protect their privacy, it is not always possible. Determined identity thieves develop skills in both hi- and low-tech ways to get what rightfully belongs to only one individual.

How Identity Thieves Get Personal Information

An identity thief is first and foremost a thief. Stealing a purse or a wallet is a low-tech, but effective, way to gain access to all of the

GETTING A ROTTEN NAME

According to the FTC, "Sitting out there on the Internet, available to anyone who knows how to get to it, or even to those who happen to stumble across it while browsing around, is plenty of personal identification information." Take, for example, the case of Thomas Seitz. While surfing the Internet one day from a computer at his public library, he found the most amazing database. It was a collection of disclosure forms that are publicly available on the Web site of the U.S. Securities and Exchange Commission (SEC). It so happens that public companies (companies that are owned by shareholders) have certain reporting obligations. This may mean that personnel who manage and operate a public company (and sometimes the shareholders) are required by law to file disclosure forms with the SEC. The information they must report varies, but could include salary, benefits, and bonuses.

This information is then made available to the public by posting it on the SEC Web site. That is where Thomas Seitz found it, and the game was on. Seitz stole the identity of one of the names in the database and used it to apply for a car loan. The Bank of America, where he had applied, rejected the application, and all of the rest of the applications he filed under the next 22 identities from the database. His 23rd attempt yielded him a $30,000 loan. Seitz planned to use the money to buy a car from a local dealership, but since he had not acquired automobile insurance (a requirement to buy a car), he changed his mind and did not make any further efforts to buy the car.

valuable personal information people carry in there. Stealing mail is another handy low-tech way for an identity thief to have a look at a wealth of useful information. This includes bank statements, credit card statements, utility bills, tax information, or pre-approved credit card offers. Filling out a quick and easy change of address form at the post office can reroute all of someone's mail to a new location. Stealing mail is less risky this way.

Finally, on his 28th attempt, Seitz hit pay dirt. Stealing the identity of Richard Clasen was easy enough. When Seitz assumed Clasen's identity and tried once again to get a loan, Bank of America issued him a check for $88,000 for the purpose of paying a car dealership for a new automobile. This time he would have insurance. Seitz used Clasen's personal identity information to get free quotes for car insurance online.

Next, Seitz went online to look for some MasterCard numbers that he could buy. Once he acquired a few of these handy numbers, he needed to be able to prove that he was, in fact, Richard Clasen. That meant he needed to have identifying documents. Another quick trip to the Internet, and he found what he needed. There are loads of Web sites out there that provide customers with all kinds of counterfeit identifying documents. It was not long until Seitz had purchased a fake birth certificate and a W-2 form that he could use to prove that he was Richard Clasen.

Now that Seitz was in the driver's seat, so to speak, he went to a local Honda dealership and found a black Prelude that he liked. But Seitz was not going to pay sticker price. He began to haggle with the salesman on the price. Not surprisingly, though, with Clausen's still-good credit, Seitz was able to get a better price for a loan than he had from Bank of America initially.

All seemed to be going Seitz's way, until he presented his phony driver's license. When the dealer began the process of registering the car, the state recognized the bogus driver's license. Seitz was caught in the act.[7]

How Identity Thieves Use Personal Information

When an identity thief has successfully rerouted a billing statement from the victim's address to his own, he can begin running up charges on the victim's account. Because the victim might not notice right away that she has not received a bill, the thief can make a lot of charges before the victim realizes there is a problem and takes action to stop any further charges from accumulating.

IDENTITY THEFT HAS REACHED CRITICAL MASS

Back in the 1990s, when identity theft first began to boom, the FTC began to collect reports of complaints and entered them into a database known as the Identity Theft Data Clearinghouse, which it continues to maintain today. The form for filing an ID Theft Complaint can be found online. As a result of tracking all of the incidents of identity theft reported, the FTC has come to realize that identity theft is continuing to increase dramatically. Consequently a growing industry has developed to help consumers protect themselves.

Identity Theft Insurance

Businesses have realized that identity theft is the fastest growing type of crime in the United States, and where there is a lot of anything, there is a lot of profit to be made. As a result, some companies will monitor or clean up an individual's credit report for a fee. According to a 2010 article in the *Hartford Courant*, "There is no question that there are a lot of identity theft victims—13 million and counting."[8]

The *Hartford Courant* also points out that "insurance companies have jumped on the bandwagon as well." These companies sell identity fraud expense coverage that claims to protect victims from the ravages of identity theft. The companies market their services to people who want to be secure in the knowledge that if they do become victims of identity theft, they will be reimbursed.

In addition, "Companies like Travelers Property Casualty Corporation sell this insurance to both corporate and personal customers." The coverage is designed to reimburse a client for the expenses involved in recovery, such as expenses incurred for travel

Stolen identities are frequently used to gain access to government benefits, such as free medical care. In July 2011, the U.S. Senate held a hearing to discuss fraud in Medicaid and Medicare. *(Source: Scott J. Ferrell/Congressional Quarterly/Getty Images)*

required to make in-person affidavits or testify in court. The coverage is not actually for the theft of personal identifying information, but for the fraud that is committed on a person or company. Furthermore, the insurance doesn't reimburse the client for what was stolen—only for what it costs to try to recover.

"As a result of their analysis on their claims data," says the *Hartford Courant*, "Travelers has stated that 76 percent of the claims they handle are a result of burglary—physical theft that includes wallets, purses, or other types of identifying information." The company uses its claims data and input from their customers to modify the types of coverage it offers.

"According to Travelers," states the *Hartford Courant*, "one of the most common claims filed by their identity theft clients is for cases of fraud that involve the use of a person's medical health insurance." Often these types of claims are filed by people who have no health insurance or who are undocumented workers with no right to health care benefits. Prosecuting these claims is extremely difficult, because getting access to the evidence of such fraud is easier said than done. The Health Insurance Portability and Accounting Act (HIPA), passed by Congress in 1996, included a provision that protects patient privacy. It is this law that makes obtaining evidence in health insurance fraud cases a thorny task.[9]

SUMMARY

In the final analysis, people can greatly decrease the risk of having their identity stolen and used for fraudulent or criminal purposes. It would be impossible, however, to guarantee that the possibility of identity theft has been completely eliminated. The best approach to managing the security of a personal identity is threefold. First, protect as well as possible the personal information that, if compromised, could open the door to identity theft. Second, stay informed about identity theft. Know how it occurs, what steps should be taken if identity theft occurs, and what avenues of help are available to victims. Finally, if a person does become a victim of identity theft, he should report the incident as soon as possible. There is no question that recovering from identity theft can be a time-consuming and costly ordeal, but being knowledgeable about how to go about it will go a long way to take the sting out of the bite.

Types and Methods of Identity Theft

American Express has a policy to immediately replace a customer's lost card, so as to minimize the problems the customer might encounter without it. So, when Lisa Ryan provided an American Express customer service representative her driver's license as proof of her identity, she received her new card promptly.

What's wrong with this story? It wasn't Lisa Ryan in the American Express (AMEX) office getting a new card. In fact, the driver's license she showed the customer service representative was a fake identity document. Yet, since the fake document went undetected and a new card was actually issued to the thief, it did not take much time until huge charges had accumulated on Lisa's AMEX account. The imposter purchased high-dollar items like appliances, expensive clothing, and valuable jewelry.

As it turned out, during the days leading up to the AMEX incident, the real Lisa Ryan had been a victim of identity theft several times over. All the money had been drained from her bank account, and her credit card was cloned and maxed out.

How did all this happen? A group of swindlers ganged up and each one got a job at some large business where they had access to personal identifying information about the business's customers. Working as a team, they managed to amass an enormous number of personal identification records (including people's credit and employment records), which they then turned into false identifications. Some of them actually sold the information on the street for $36 a pop. With the rest of the information, they managed to average around $29,000 per victim in fraudulent credit card charges. This gang of con artists was eventually caught and brought to justice. But for Lisa Ryan, it was too late. It took her more than a year to clean up the mess. [1]

The preceding case is one example of identity theft, but there are many other means to pulling off this crime. Identity thieves can be persistent and inventive in finding ways to exploit data and financial systems.

THREE BASIC TYPES OF IDENTITY THEFT

Lisa's problem was a classic case of organized identity theft perpetrated to achieve financial gain. It is representative of the first of three categories into which cases of identity theft are classified:

1. Financial
2. Criminal
3. Identity assumption

Financial

Identity theft can be an easy path to fast money. Identity theft for the purposes of financial gain is a big problem and getting bigger all the time. One reason for this is that it is much easier (and usually safer) to steal someone's purse or wallet than it is to rob a convenience store. It is much easier for a gang of con men (or women) to quickly throw together a scheme to get a lot of identities to sell than to rob a casino. For example, think of the movies *Ocean's Eleven* and *Ocean's Twelve*. There was a lot of expensive work in those heists,

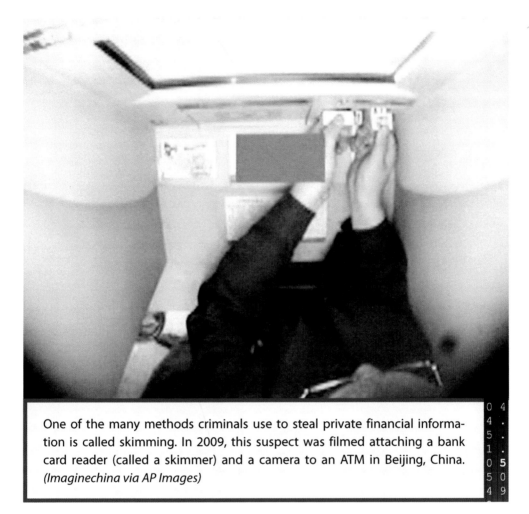

One of the many methods criminals use to steal private financial information is called skimming. In 2009, this suspect was filmed attaching a bank
card reader (called a skimmer) and a camera to an ATM in Beijing, China.
(Imaginechina via AP Images)

even though they were a work of fiction, and they made it look easy
to do the crime. In reality, pulling off such heists is risky and likely
to draw immediate attention from the police. Compare that to the
people in Lisa Ryan's case, who just got jobs with access to sensitive
material and even got paid to do their dirty work.[2]

Criminal

According to the Privacy Rights Clearinghouse (a project of the
Utility Consumers' Action Network [UCAN], an American nonprofit consumer advocacy organization), "Criminal identity theft

WHEN FINANCIAL IDENTITY THEFT HITS CLOSE TO HOME

Talk about betrayal. According to the Identity Theft Assistance Center, which provides victim assistance and identity management services, "When Amanda, a 63-year-old tax preparer, received a statement with $5,000 in charges on her GM MasterCard, she recognized the fact that someone was using her identity." She did not have a GM MasterCard and had never even applied for one. When she contacted HSBC, the bank that issued the card, they confirmed what she suspected: She had become a victim of identity theft.

Once investigators started checking into it, they found out that the thief had been using her identity for some time. There was also another account number in Amanda's name that she had never opened. Someone had made five other attempts to open new accounts.

For Amanda, it was a no-brainer as to who was the most likely person to have stolen her identity. She and her husband Joe had

has very serious, scary consequences." It is bad enough if a person steals someone's identity to get money; but imagine the consequences to the victim if an identity thief uses a stolen persona to commit crimes. The thief gets away while an innocent person is left to take the blame. The victim may be arrested, charged, and even prosecuted, without even knowing about the theft of his identity.[3]

Alternately, the victim might be hurt by a hidden criminal record associated with his identity. For example, an identity theft victim may find it harder to find a job. When a prospective employer rented out an apartment on their premises to a young man with three small sons. Amanda and Joe had become quite fond of the young father and his children, and they treated him much like a son. The small family visited them quite often in Amanda and Joe's home, where they often used her computer.

Amanda felt betrayed, and sickened by what she knew must have happened. She filed a police report and sure enough, investigators found her mail in her tenant's apartment. She and Joe evicted their tenant—the man they had cared so much about. When he tried to reenter the apartment, they had to file a restraining order. Amanda and Joe felt compassion for the young man who had gone so sadly off course, but they had no choice. They had to protect themselves.

Amanda learned her lesson the hard way. She no longer gives her trust to people, no matter who they are. She most certainly will never let anyone use her computer again. And, she has deleted software from her computer that automatically completes online purchase applications. That software automatically inserted the last four digits of her Social Security number into applications, making it simple for her tenant to steal her identity.[4]

does a background check on the applicant and finds that he has a criminal history, chances are they will not hire him. The victim might not even know the record exists. Potential employers, however, must get permission from applicants to check their credit history, and the law requires that they then inform the applicants if a bad credit report was a factor in not hiring them. This may be how the victim finally learns what has been going on in his name. The FTC explains this process online at: http://ftc.gov/documents/bus08-using-consumer-reports-what-employers-need-to-know.[5]

Identity Assumption

Identity assumption is a bit different. In identity theft, there is usually a financial motive to the crime. Identity assumption, on the other hand, is quite frequently both personal and malicious. The thief wants to hurt a particular victim for some personal reason, such as revenge. The perpetrator may be close enough to the victim (at least physically) to gather the information needed to pull off something mean and hateful. They might pose online as the victim and post negative or obscene things about the victim's friends or family, things that are untrue or unflattering or even sensitive, personal pictures. It often works. It can be devastating to the victim to learn that someone dislikes them so much that they would do something to embarrass or destroy them. It is not only the personal pain that the victim might suffer, however, but also the continued frustration of such information being online under their name, because it can be very difficult to completely delete things from the Internet.

Other Types of Identity Assumption

There are other types of identity assumption that are not necessarily motivated by malice, but they can be just as harmful to the victim. There are millions of illegal immigrants in the United States. They come here seeking employment but are unable to obtain citizenship. That makes them potential customers for stolen identities. According to the Identity Theft Resource Center, "Illegal immigrants are potential customers for stolen identities, which they use to get jobs and health benefits illegally."[6] In the process they damage the credit history of the person whose identity they assume.

USING BIRTH CERTIFICATES FOR FRAUD

Some identity thieves have made such a mess of their financial lives that they decide to start over by using someone else's identification. These thieves sometimes target the identity of a deceased child. Regular perusal of old newspapers or death certificates (sometimes available on the Internet) often yields such names. Picking out someone approximately the thief's age and same sex is easy enough.

Then all the thief has to do is to counterfeit some documents or even purchase a replacement birth certificate through the system and he can become someone else.[7]

According to Adoption Media, LLC (a group committed to helping as many children as possible find permanent homes), "People routinely need to get copies of birth certificates to show proof that an event did occur." A person may have lost the birth certificates; or they were burned in a fire; or, maybe they are just buried so deep in a person's files that no one knows where to look for them. Regardless of the scenario, when something comes up in a person's life that requires proof of these events, the official copies must be obtained. Consequently, each state and the United States territories have some kind of centralized clearing house of such documents, generally called the Vital Statistics Bureau. Each state establishes the requirements for legally obtaining copies of official records and the fees for getting copies of the documents.[8]

A call to the vital statistics department in the state where a person was born will yield information about what identification is required for a new birth certificate. There is also a helpful document on the Internet, maintained by the Centers for Disease Control and Prevention (CDC) on their Web site, with information about each state's requirements and fees: http://www.cdc.gov/nchs/w2w.htm.[9]

CHILD AND TEEN IDENTITY THEFT

Children and teens are extremely vulnerable to identity theft. By virtue of the fact that children's credit reports are usually pristine, they are greatly desirable to identity thieves. In fact, child identity theft is increasing exponentially, even if statisticians cannot really estimate accurately because so many of the crimes remain undetected at present. "The FTC believes that as many as 7 percent of identity thieves target children. That number could be approaching a million cases out there involving children and teens."[10] The Identity Theft Resource Center indicates that "in 56 percent of their child identity theft cases, the victim was a child under the age of six."[11, 12] Most creditors do not verify an applicant's age, which allows identity thieves to use the identity of even a small child. This puts children and teens at special risk.

WHY CHILD AND TEEN IDENTITY THEFT MATTERS

Considering how simple it often is for someone who wants it to get another person's identity, especially the identity of a child in the thief's extended family, it isn't surprising that it happens. According to John Sileo, "Once the thief has the identity, he or she can use it for their own purchases, extra cash, even to rent or purchase housing."[13]

The FTC reports that 700,000 children have their identities stolen every year, and the numbers are rising. This means that as these youngsters come of age and try to enter the financial world, they will be severely hampered by their ravaged credit reports. In those kinds of numbers, the fact that these young people have trouble getting school and car loans, credit cards, driver's licenses, bank accounts, and many other aspects of the economy, the community at large is also crippled financially. Furthermore, when young people must spend their time unraveling a torn and tattered credit report, they are not spending their time well. The community and the country suffer for their difficult start in life.[14]

COMMON METHODS TO GET IDENTITY INFORMATION

Some of the most common methods criminals use to get a person's critical identifying information are:

- shoulder surfing
- skimming
- dumpster diving
- taking advantage of offers
- fraudulent e-mail or phishing

Shoulder Surfing

Shoulder surfing is a method of stealing a person's identity. The thief watches a person who is performing a transaction at an ATM or inputting their personal identification number (PIN) when paying

After a seven-year struggle, Chip St. Clair was still trying to clear up his credit history in 2005. His parents had stolen his identity and accrued debt under his name and Social Security number. *(AP Photo/Jerry S. Mendoza)*

for a purchase. He makes a note of the number and any other personal information that might be exposed during the transaction.[15]

Skimming

Skimming can refer to thieves using electronic devices to record customer information at ATM machines, but it also happens during routine credit card transactions. An employee sometimes takes a customer's card out of sight to run the transaction. Paying for dinner at a restaurant is a good example, but it could happen at a clothing shop or any other type of business. While the card is out of sight, the identity thief, taking advantage of his position, records the card information and the customer's personal data for later use.[16]

Dumpster Diving

Dumpster diving, or going through someone's garbage, is a method of gaining access to useful personal identification information. It may seem distasteful, but it is popular among identity thieves. If a victim discards items, such as credit card billing statements or pre-approved credit card offers, without destroying them, then an identity thief can retrieve it from the trash and use it.[17]

Taking Advantage of Offers

Some identity thieves look into a person's mailbox to acquire information about a person's business and personal activities. They can read bank statements, credit card statements, and other personal documents found in the victim's mail. It also allows the thief the opportunity to open pre-approved credit cards that banks send out, which they can use to open fraudulent accounts.[18]

Fraudulent E-mail or Phishing

A clever method of getting useful information from potential victims involves the use of fraudulent e-mails to get a victim to willingly send the thief their passwords, account numbers, social security numbers, and other types of information. Commonly referred to as phishing, the thief sends out e-mails purporting to be someone the victim will trust, like a bank or a credit card company.[19] The e-mail prompts the victim to update his account or confirm a transaction by replying with personal information or by filling out an online form. Any information provided goes straight to an identity thief.

SUMMARY

Using a false identity in the commission of a crime is a federal crime. When a thief steals someone's personal identification information and uses it (whether for financial gain, for deception, to hurt someone for revenge, to elude the law, or just to live a life that they could not live otherwise), it is called "identity theft." There are millions of incidents of identity theft each year, and the numbers are rising. It is a crime that is particularly pernicious because victims of identity theft may not only lose money and be denied credit for goods and services, but they also lose a chunk of their life that must be devoted to recovery. Furthermore the losses to businesses and to individuals are astronomical.[20]

Minimizing Risk

According to Halifax (a U.K.-based bank), "Celena, a 21-year-old assistant manager, never gave any thought to identity fraud." It just didn't seem to have anything to do with her. Then one day she received an e-mail that took her by surprise: Her credit card application was being processed. She knew that someone was using her identity because she hadn't applied for a credit card. Celena immediately contacted the bank and canceled the application.

Unfortunately, that was just the beginning of Celena's problems. The identity thief who had stolen Celena's identity had a lot of her personal information and was using it to apply for loans and other credit cards. Now, Celena thought about identity fraud a lot, because she was spending a lot of time canceling applications. She couldn't help but worry about whether her personal identifying information was being used in some way that she couldn't know about. She filed the proper reports, but the local police were pretty busy and didn't make any progress on her case.

As an added security measure, Celena hired a company to monitor her credit report, but there were new applications coming in as time went on. The agency Celena had hired was able to help get a note attached to her credit report explaining the situation, so that credit she wanted to get for herself wouldn't be jeopardized. The attack on Celena's identity was a wake-up call. Now she is very careful to protect her private information from prying eyes and she continues to pay close attention to her credit report.[1]

While identity theft may not always be prevented, anyone can minimize the risk by managing personal information wisely. It is extremely difficult, if not impossible, to completely protect an

In 2011, 18-year-old Jake Davis was arrested and charged with being linked to online hacking groups such as LulzSec and Anonymous. These international groups are known for disabling government Web sites and accessing personal user information from corporations. *(Rex Features via AP Images)*

identity. There are simply too many ways that it is exposed in the ordinary business of day-to-day life to completely avoid becoming a victim. It is almost impossible to get through life in the United States without a Social Security number. Or, imagine paying for everything with cash. It wouldn't be impossible, but in today's world, it would prevent a person from having and doing a lot of the things that are a normal part of life. For example, in case of an accident, it is not easy to forego a trip to the hospital. Also, it is impossible to make online purchases with cash.

No person or company is entirely safe from identity theft. Even high-tech corporations with plenty of security resources are vulnerable. In April and October 2011, Sony's PlayStation network was attacked by hackers. The thieves shut down the PlayStation network, a system that links online-gaming units and allows players to purchase additional games, and gained access to credit card and other personal information from millions of customers. Other companies that have experienced high-profile security breaches include Citigroup, attacked in June 2011, leading to information from more than 200,000 accounts being exposed, and the RSA Security Division of the EMC Company, breached in March 2011, compromising security products in use by many companies and government agencies.

THE HOWS OF PROTECTING YOURSELF AGAINST IDENTITY THEFT

No matter how careful a person might be, there is always a chance that an identity will be stolen by a very determined thief. Awareness of the risk of identity theft and knowing how to spot it are two key steps in lowering the risk. One basic means of protection is to carefully monitor credit reports for suspicious activity. Sometimes the risk of identity theft is more immediate, however, such as when an individual loses a wallet or purse.

Losing a Wallet or Purse

People typically carry plenty of personal information in their wallet or their purse. They might have a driver's license, a credit card or a bank debit card, a health insurance card, a school ID, or any

TESTING THE IDENTITY THEFT QUOTIENT

How much information does a person need to know about identity theft to be protected? Here is a quick quiz from the Privacy Rights Clearinghouse (a nonprofit consumer organization that provides consumer information and consumer advocacy) to test the Identity Quotient, as shown in Table 3.1.[2]

TABLE 3.1 TESTING THE IDENTITY QUOTIENT.		
STATEMENT	TRUE	FALSE
Identity theft happens to older people who have a lot of credit cards.		
It is safe to use the Internet without antivirus software or another form of online protection.		
People can't see a PIN number when people are entering it on a keypad.		
Banks and other companies sometimes request a customer's password via e-mail.		
It isn't necessary to have a locked mailbox.		
It isn't important to check credit reports regularly for unexplained activity.		
Privacy settings in online social networks fully protect users' personal information.		
People don't dig around in trash to find identifying information.		
It is a good idea to carry a Social Security card in a purse or wallet.		
Shredding personal mail and identifying information is not necessary.		
Having a Social Security number on an ID badge that is worn in public is okay.		
It is not important to keep personal information out of sight in the home.		

(continues)

(continued)

According to the Privacy Rights Clearinghouse, "A person who answers false to all the questions above is less likely to become a victim of identity theft." People who think that any of the above statements are true are very likely to become a victim of identity theft.[3]

number of other personal documents. This is a veritable gold mine of information for identity thieves. If the person happens to be carrying a Social Security card, it is a cinch for an identity thief to take over. The only bright spot in this scenario is that people often know almost immediately about a missing purse or wallet, giving them warning so they can contact the bank and credit card companies to report the loss. Even if the wallet or purse is returned seemingly intact, consideration should be given to at least requesting replacement cards, unless there is no doubt about where the item was while it was missing.

TABLE 3.2 TYPICAL WALLET CONTENTS	
COMMON CONTENTS	**ADDITIONAL CONTENTS**
• driver's license or state-issued photo identification	• medical insurance card
• credit and debit cards	• auto insurance card
• checkbook	• student or military identification
• ATM cards	• bus and train cards
• phone cards	• personal photos
• Social Security card	• other permits and licenses
• various other membership cards	• birth certificate, passport, or visa
	• receipts and bank statements

Do people really need to carry all that personal identifying information everywhere they go? Probably not. Consider reorganizing or sorting a wallet or purse to reduce the personal information it contains. Nevertheless, vigilance in watching over personal property carried on one's person is always needed.

Warning! PDAs and Cell Phones

Smart phones are a great way to store a lot of information; doing this eliminates the need to carry many of the identification items typically found in a wallet or purse. Most handheld or mobile digital devices will work to record data. However, a cell phone can be lost too. If personal information is stored in a cell phone or any other digital device, the device should be password protected so that a person who finds the device will not be able to use it. Also make sure to back up all data stored on the device.

AVOIDING IDENTITY THEFT

People can do a few things to limit their exposure to identity theft criminals. In some cases a parent may need to take action on behalf of their children. The following items can also help increase awareness of the different types of identity theft:

- Open a credit report for a child and request that a "freeze" be put on it until a child is ready to use credit.
- Do not leave mail sitting in mailboxes longer than necessary.
- Do not reply to e-mails asking for any kind of account or password information.
- Monitor credit reports regularly so that in the event of identity theft, the damage can be stopped sooner than later.
- Shield entry of PINs from possible recording by hidden cameras.[4]

SAFEGUARDING SOCIAL SECURITY NUMBERS

According to the FTC, "There are legitimate reasons for an organization to know a person's Social Security Number." Sometimes it is

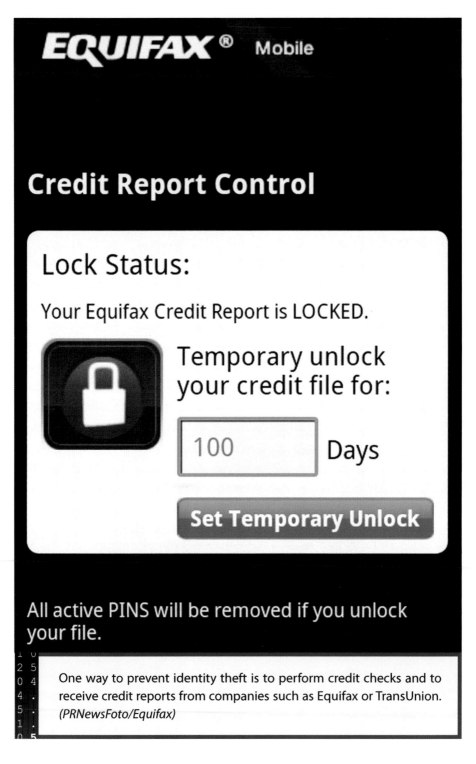

One way to prevent identity theft is to perform credit checks and to receive credit reports from companies such as Equifax or TransUnion. *(PRNewsFoto/Equifax)*

not necessary for a company to have a person's SSN to perform their service or provide goods to their customers. Some companies ask for the number as a form of identification or for their record keeping. People should consider carefully when entering into a business relationship with a company whether or not they really need to turn over their Social Security number. When a person is asked in the course of initiating a relationship with a new business to provide a Social Security number, he should ask:

- What will happen if the SSN is not surrendered?
- Why is the SSN required?
- How will the SSN be used?
- Does the law require the use of the SSN?[5]

MINIMIZING RISK BY GUARDING AGAINST IDENTITY THEFT

Once all steps have been taken to protect information, consider using a credit report and monitoring service. Everyone is busy and life just takes over, so rather than risking an unintended failure to monitor accounts personally, take advantage of services that will review a credit report on a regular schedule and let the customer know if something fishy turns up. This is especially useful if a person is at higher risk for identity theft; if, for instance, they have a number of credit cards, or if there has already been a threat to information security. The first step in putting a stop to an identity theft campaign is knowing about it.[6]

SUMMARY

Identity theft is fast becoming one of the major problems of the 21st century. The risks of having a person's identity stolen and misused are clear, and they are hidden in day-to-day transactions undertaken by people in the ordinary business of conducting their lives. Transactions like using a debit card at a fast food restaurant, paying for groceries with an ATM card, or shopping online for that new best seller may leave a person exposed to an identity thief. So, it stands to reason that taking precautions to minimize the risk of identity theft is a good practice.[7] The best protection is awareness of the risk of identity theft, careful monitoring of credit reports and personal accounts, minimizing personal information carried in a wallet or purse, and being cautious when sharing a Social Security number.

best way to detect identity theft early is to monitor credit reports on a routine basis. Even though monitoring credit reports on young children may seem unnecessary, it should also be done to be sure that there is no credit history before there should be one.[3] It is also a good idea to regularly check bank and credit card accounts online. Fraudulent activity can show up there within a day or two, which means the customer can alert the financial institution right away.

Get Free Annual Credit Reports

According to Jonathan Citrin of the investment company Citrin-Group, "People are entitled to get a free copy of their credit report once a year from each of the three major reporting agencies." These are Equifax, Experian, and TransUnion. Credit reports can be viewed online where information will be sorted into seven sections in the report:

- personal information
- account information
- inquiries
- collections
- public records
- consumer statement
- dispute file information[4]

Take the time to read each report carefully. Make a note of anything that seems wrong, even if it might appear to be insignificant. Then let the credit-reporting agency know immediately so that it can be corrected. Even a slight error could indicate a problem.[5]

According to Securian Financial Group, Inc., "Federal law provides that a person is entitled to get a free copy of their credit report if they are turned down for a credit application, or other things like insurance or employment." These are called "adverse actions." In order to take advantage of this law, one must write to the credit bureau requesting a free copy of their credit report within 60 days of receiving notice of adverse action.[6]

4

Detecting, Reporting, and Recovering from Identity Theft

According to ID Watchdog, Inc. (a company that provides protection services to consumers), when Gloria Neece tried to open a new credit account she was declined, despite what she knew to be her good financial history. She had been very careful to build it precisely so that she would have no trouble getting credit when she needed it. And, when she was ready to reap the reward of her careful planning, she couldn't get the credit she had counted on for her and her fiancé to buy a new house together. The timing was awful. She was about to be deployed to Afghanistan.

Being declined was her first clue that her identity had been stolen. The problem didn't stop there. Almost immediately, Gloria began to receive the first of many calls from creditors trying to collect on debts she had never incurred on accounts she had never opened.

Because Gloria is basically a take-charge kind of gal, she was inclined to start making the necessary calls and taking on the tasks that would be needed to clear her name. But, the time spent on the telephone and filling out forms was nipping into her little remaining time, so she changed her plan and sought the aid of legal counsel.

Luckily, the legal counsel was well versed in identity theft and had access to professional identity theft experts. The team had Gloria put together a list of the unrecognized addresses that were popping up in her credit reports. From there, the team discovered that there was additional derogatory information on her credit report: a fraudulent medical bill, an unauthorized bank account, and a criminal offense record that Gloria knew nothing about.

Gloria went to Afghanistan, not sure of what to expect when she returned. But, while Gloria was gone, the identity theft team got to work on the recovery process for her. They contacted the fraud departments of the creditors and disputed the account and charges. They cleared her of the fraudulent debt for medical services. They used a Limited Power of Attorney to get her record expunged of the criminal offense. When Gloria left, her credit score was drowning in the upper 400s. When she returned, the number had soared back to the upper 700s; and she and her fiancé are well on their way to home ownership.[1]

As Gloria found out, there are clear signs when a person's identity has been stolen and used in fraudulent ways. According to Securian Financial Group, Inc. (providers of financial security for individuals and businesses in the form of insurance, retirement plans, and investments), some of those signs are:

- Learning about accounts and debts that one never opened or incurred
- Finding inaccurate information on one's credit report, such as incorrect addresses or employers
- Noticing that monthly statements have not shown up as usual
- Being unable to obtain credit or being offered credit terms that have a high interest rate
- Receiving debt collection telephone calls or letters for unknown purchases or debts[2]

After discovering someone was using her Social Security number, this victim of identity theft filed a police report and began collecting information on the credit card accounts she supposedly opened. *(AP Photo/Gene Blythe)*

PERSONAL INFORMATION SHOULD BE MONITORED REGULARLY

It is clear that the earlier the detection of identity theft occurs, the better the opportunity to stop it before it creates a nightmare. The

Using Credit Monitoring Services

A service that accepts the responsibility to monitor people's credit reports for a fee is known as a credit monitoring service. These services are offered by the credit reporting agencies, banks, and some independent companies.[7] According to Check-your-credit-score .com (credit-score checking and repair service), "A credit monitoring service may make life a bit simpler by doing a routine financial chore that people would otherwise need to do themselves." People use services all the time to do many other kinds of chores they would rather not spend time doing (take lawn services, for example).[8]

IDENTITY THEFT REPORTING AND RECOVERING

According to Money-Zine.com, (a source for financial planning, career development, and investment information), "Recent statistics

FRAUD ALERT

According to the Privacy Rights Clearinghouse, "A fraud alert is designed to help protect individuals who have reason to suspect that their identity has been compromised (for example, in the event of the loss of a wallet or purse)." An individual can place a fraud alert on a person's account. The initial fraud alert will remain on the credit report for at least 90 days, and it can be renewed if necessary. It works to alert creditors that special precautions must be taken in handling credit applications in the individual's name. This usually involves a phone call to the individual at their established home or work phone number. There is no requirement, however, that a person has to be a potential victim of identity theft to place the alert, and having an alert on a credit report is great (and free!) protection. Of course, in the event a person actually needs to obtain credit during the period of the fraud alert, having an alert could be problematic.[9]

on identity theft show that almost 30 million people become victims each year; and, that trend is increasing at a distressing rate." It is obvious that the amount of money lost to thieves from these many incidents is serious. When this kind of money is at stake, the federal government wants to be sure that they know about it for a lot of reasons, one of which is to help victims recover. There are three primary concerns of an identity theft victim:

- Stopping the identity thief from any further use of the stolen identity.
- Helping law enforcement catch the thief by providing pertinent information.
- Initiating the recovery process.[10]

Documenting Identity Theft

A good memory is no substitute for good documentation when it comes to identity theft. The process of reporting and recovery is something that takes place over time, and it is unlikely that anyone could remember the details that might eventually be needed. Consequently, a victim should be aware from the very start that it is imperative to accurately and precisely document their case by:

- *Establishing a file.* The file will provide a physical holding space separate from any other paperwork on other subjects. As the case progresses, there will be paperwork that results from the steps the victim takes toward recovery.
- *Establishing a journal.* In identity theft cases, telephone calls are usually the first form of communication between the victim and the various stakeholders involved in the case. The victim should make a record that the call took place as part of the documentation that may be required at some stage of the journey to recovery.

CREDIT REPORTING AGENCIES

There are three major credit reporting agencies. All three maintain a credit report on every individual's financial history, starting with the first use of the individual's Social Security number in the financial system. The data in each agency's credit report on an individual may not be exactly the same, because different businesses and organizations may report financial transactions to only one or another of the agencies. Be sure to work with all three of these agencies when there has been an incident of fraud, or when an identity has been stolen. The credit reporting agencies are a great source of information and help on identity theft:

Equifax
P.O. Box 740241
Atlanta, GA 30374-0241
Toll-Free Number: 1-888-202-4025
http://www.equifax.com

Experian
P.O. Box 9532
Allen, TX 75013
Toll-Free Number: 1-888-397-3742
http://www.experian.com

TransUnion
Fraud Victim Assistance Division
P.O. Box 6790
Fullerton, CA 92834-6790
Toll-Free Number: 1-800-680-7289
http://www.transunion.com

- *Using written communication.* Telephone calls and personal conversations are great to speed up the process of stopping the thief from doing further damage, but in legal cases, written proof does the heavy lifting. Be sure to follow up on every phone call or personal conversation in writing to stakeholders, legal representatives, and organizations involved in the case, and keep copies.
- *Organizing the case file.* As the file on the case grows, organize it so that it tells a story. The way the material is organized should be meaningful to the victim, so that referring back to phone calls and events is a simple task.[11]

Identity Theft Reports

To dispute fraudulent charges on an account, an individual will need to provide more than their word to the credit reporting agencies that the charges were the result of identity theft. One of the primary reasons why identity theft must be reported is to document the fact that a theft has occurred. A copy of a police report or an identity theft report is required to prove to credit reporting agencies that an individual has been a victim of identity theft. If reporting the crime is not a matter of urgency, it is useful to start by preparing the identity theft report first, by using the FTC's Identity Theft Complaint Form, which can be found online at https://www.ftccomplaintassistant.gov/FTC_Wizard.aspx?Lang=en. This will help the victim capture specific details regarding the incident. This documentation allows easy filing of a report with the police, because the information needed is readily available. The victim should ask that this form be appended to the standard police report. A comprehensive identity theft report should have two parts:

- The first part contains information, such as the date the identity theft took place (if it is known), any information about the identity thief that the victim may have, and a listing of accounts that have fallen prey to fraudulent activity.

UNITED STATES

FEDERAL
TRADE
COMMISSION
BUILDING

VISITORS ENTRANCE
6TH & PENN. AVE
6 ENTRANCE
7TH & PENN. AVE

The Federal Trade Commission provides a form for victims of identity theft to document the specifics of the crime. The completed form, known as the identity theft report, can be attached to a police report. *(Source: AP Photo/ Elswick)*

- The second part contains more detailed information that creditors may need in order to take further action toward prosecution and recovery.[12]

Other steps to take once identity theft is uncovered are

- Contact the bank immediately if a debit card or check-book was lost.
- Contact credit card companies if credit cards or other charge cards were lost or stolen. Some credit card companies have a method of picking out unusual spending patterns on a particular account, which may alert them to the potential of fraudulent spending.
- Contact an insurance agent. Homeowners may be covered for identity theft by their homeowners' insurance.
- Get a new driver's license if one was lost or stolen. Notify the Bureau of Motor Vehicles and obtain a new one with a new number rather than a duplicate copy of the old one.
- Change locks if keys were lost or stolen.
- Call other card issuers to report the loss or theft of library cards, movie rental cards, gym membership cards, health insurance cards, and other types of membership cards. Notify any business or organization in which one has a membership that extends credit or permits the use of a private facility.
- Call a lawyer. Whether or not an identity theft victim will require legal services to recover their identity depends on the type and extent of the damage they have experienced, but it's good to consult a lawyer early in the process.

SUMMARY

According to Jonathan Citrin, "When it comes to identity theft, the ideal situation is to prevent it." If prevention does not succeed in staving off the thieves, then the next best thing is to be quick about

Detecting, Reporting, and Recovering from Identity Theft

According to ID Watchdog, Inc. (a company that provides protection services to consumers), when Gloria Neece tried to open a new credit account she was declined, despite what she knew to be her good financial history. She had been very careful to build it precisely so that she would have no trouble getting credit when she needed it. And, when she was ready to reap the reward of her careful planning, she couldn't get the credit she had counted on for her and her fiancé to buy a new house together. The timing was awful. She was about to be deployed to Afghanistan.

Being declined was her first clue that her identity had been stolen. The problem didn't stop there. Almost immediately, Gloria began to receive the first of many calls from creditors trying to collect on debts she had never incurred on accounts she had never opened.

Because Gloria is basically a take-charge kind of gal, she was inclined to start making the necessary calls and taking on the tasks that would be needed to clear her name. But, the time spent on the telephone and filling out forms was nipping into her little remaining time, so she changed her plan and sought the aid of legal counsel.

Luckily, the legal counsel was well versed in identity theft and had access to professional identity theft experts. The team had Gloria put together a list of the unrecognized addresses that were popping up in her credit reports. From there, the team discovered that there was additional derogatory information on her credit report: a fraudulent medical bill, an unauthorized bank account, and a criminal offense record that Gloria knew nothing about.

Gloria went to Afghanistan, not sure of what to expect when she returned. But, while Gloria was gone, the identity theft team got to work on the recovery process for her. They contacted the fraud departments of the creditors and disputed the account and charges. They cleared her of the fraudulent debt for medical services. They used a Limited Power of Attorney to get her record expunged of the criminal offense. When Gloria left, her credit score was drowning in the upper 400s. When she returned, the number had soared back to the upper 700s; and she and her fiancé are well on their way to home ownership.[1]

As Gloria found out, there are clear signs when a person's identity has been stolen and used in fraudulent ways. According to Securian Financial Group, Inc. (providers of financial security for individuals and businesses in the form of insurance, retirement plans, and investments), some of those signs are:

- Learning about accounts and debts that one never opened or incurred
- Finding inaccurate information on one's credit report, such as incorrect addresses or employers
- Noticing that monthly statements have not shown up as usual
- Being unable to obtain credit or being offered credit terms that have a high interest rate
- Receiving debt collection telephone calls or letters for unknown purchases or debts[2]

After discovering someone was using her Social Security number, this victim of identity theft filed a police report and began collecting information on the credit card accounts she supposedly opened. *(AP Photo/Gene Blythe)*

PERSONAL INFORMATION SHOULD BE MONITORED REGULARLY

It is clear that the earlier the detection of identity theft occurs, the better the opportunity to stop it before it creates a nightmare. The best way to detect identity theft early is to monitor credit reports on a routine basis. Even though monitoring credit reports on young children may seem unnecessary, it should also be done to be sure that there is no credit history before there should be one.[3] It is also a good idea to regularly check bank and credit card accounts online. Fraudulent activity can show up there within a day or two, which means the customer can alert the financial institution right away.

Get Free Annual Credit Reports

According to Jonathan Citrin of the investment company Citrin-Group, "People are entitled to get a free copy of their credit report once a year from each of the three major reporting agencies." These are Equifax, Experian, and TransUnion. Credit reports can be viewed online where information will be sorted into seven sections in the report:

- personal information
- account information
- inquiries
- collections
- public records
- consumer statement
- dispute file information[4]

Take the time to read each report carefully. Make a note of anything that seems wrong, even if it might appear to be insignificant. Then let the credit-reporting agency know immediately so that it can be corrected. Even a slight error could indicate a problem.[5]

According to Securian Financial Group, Inc., "Federal law provides that a person is entitled to get a free copy of their credit report if they are turned down for a credit application, or other things like insurance or employment." These are called "adverse actions." In order to take advantage of this law, one must write to the credit bureau requesting a free copy of their credit report within 60 days of receiving notice of adverse action.[6]

Using Credit Monitoring Services

A service that accepts the responsibility to monitor people's credit reports for a fee is known as a credit monitoring service. These services are offered by the credit reporting agencies, banks, and some independent companies.[7] According to Check-your-credit-score .com (credit-score checking and repair service), "A credit monitoring service may make life a bit simpler by doing a routine financial chore that people would otherwise need to do themselves." People use services all the time to do many other kinds of chores they would rather not spend time doing (take lawn services, for example).[8]

IDENTITY THEFT REPORTING AND RECOVERING

According to Money-Zine.com, (a source for financial planning, career development, and investment information), "Recent statistics

FRAUD ALERT

According to the Privacy Rights Clearinghouse, "A fraud alert is designed to help protect individuals who have reason to suspect that their identity has been compromised (for example, in the event of the loss of a wallet or purse)." An individual can place a fraud alert on a person's account. The initial fraud alert will remain on the credit report for at least 90 days, and it can be renewed if necessary. It works to alert creditors that special precautions must be taken in handling credit applications in the individual's name. This usually involves a phone call to the individual at their established home or work phone number. There is no requirement, however, that a person has to be a potential victim of identity theft to place the alert, and having an alert on a credit report is great (and free!) protection. Of course, in the event a person actually needs to obtain credit during the period of the fraud alert, having an alert could be problematic.[9]

on identity theft show that almost 30 million people become victims each year; and, that trend is increasing at a distressing rate." It is obvious that the amount of money lost to thieves from these many incidents is serious. When this kind of money is at stake, the federal government wants to be sure that they know about it for a lot of reasons, one of which is to help victims recover. There are three primary concerns of an identity theft victim:

- Stopping the identity thief from any further use of the stolen identity.
- Helping law enforcement catch the thief by providing pertinent information.
- Initiating the recovery process.[10]

Documenting Identity Theft

A good memory is no substitute for good documentation when it comes to identity theft. The process of reporting and recovery is something that takes place over time, and it is unlikely that anyone could remember the details that might eventually be needed. Consequently, a victim should be aware from the very start that it is imperative to accurately and precisely document their case by:

- *Establishing a file.* The file will provide a physical holding space separate from any other paperwork on other subjects. As the case progresses, there will be paperwork that results from the steps the victim takes toward recovery.
- *Establishing a journal.* In identity theft cases, telephone calls are usually the first form of communication between the victim and the various stakeholders involved in the case. The victim should make a record that the call took place as part of the documentation that may be required at some stage of the journey to recovery.

CREDIT
REPORTING AGENCIES

There are three major credit reporting agencies. All three maintain a credit report on every individual's financial history, starting with the first use of the individual's Social Security number in the financial system. The data in each agency's credit report on an individual may not be exactly the same, because different businesses and organizations may report financial transactions to only one or another of the agencies. Be sure to work with all three of these agencies when there has been an incident of fraud, or when an identity has been stolen. The credit reporting agencies are a great source of information and help on identity theft:

Equifax
P.O. Box 740241
Atlanta, GA 30374-0241
Toll-Free Number: 1-888-202-4025
http://www.equifax.com

Experian
P.O. Box 9532
Allen, TX 75013
Toll-Free Number: 1-888-397-3742
http://www.experian.com

TransUnion
Fraud Victim Assistance Division
P.O. Box 6790
Fullerton, CA 92834-6790
Toll-Free Number: 1-800-680-7289
http://www.transunion.com

- *Using written communication.* Telephone calls and personal conversations are great to speed up the process of stopping the thief from doing further damage, but in legal cases, written proof does the heavy lifting. Be sure to follow up on every phone call or personal conversation in writing to stakeholders, legal representatives, and organizations involved in the case, and keep copies.
- *Organizing the case file.* As the file on the case grows, organize it so that it tells a story. The way the material is organized should be meaningful to the victim, so that referring back to phone calls and events is a simple task.[11]

Identity Theft Reports

To dispute fraudulent charges on an account, an individual will need to provide more than their word to the credit reporting agencies that the charges were the result of identity theft. One of the primary reasons why identity theft must be reported is to document the fact that a theft has occurred. A copy of a police report or an identity theft report is required to prove to credit reporting agencies that an individual has been a victim of identity theft. If reporting the crime is not a matter of urgency, it is useful to start by preparing the identity theft report first, by using the FTC's Identity Theft Complaint Form, which can be found online at https://www.ftccomplaintassistant.gov/FTC_Wizard.aspx?Lang=en. This will help the victim capture specific details regarding the incident. This documentation allows easy filing of a report with the police, because the information needed is readily available. The victim should ask that this form be appended to the standard police report. A comprehensive identity theft report should have two parts:

- The first part contains information, such as the date the identity theft took place (if it is known), any information about the identity thief that the victim may have, and a listing of accounts that have fallen prey to fraudulent activity.

UNITED STATES

FEDERAL
TRADE
COMMISSION
BUILDING

VISITORS ENTRANCE
6TH & PENN. AVE
& ENTRANCE
7TH & PENN. AVE

The Federal Trade Commission provides a form for victims of identity theft to document the specifics of the crime. The completed form, known as the identity theft report, can be attached to a police report. *(Source: AP Photo/ Elswick)*

- The second part contains more detailed information that creditors may need in order to take further action toward prosecution and recovery.[12]

Other steps to take once identity theft is uncovered are

- Contact the bank immediately if a debit card or checkbook was lost.
- Contact credit card companies if credit cards or other charge cards were lost or stolen. Some credit card companies have a method of picking out unusual spending patterns on a particular account, which may alert them to the potential of fraudulent spending.
- Contact an insurance agent. Homeowners may be covered for identity theft by their homeowners' insurance.
- Get a new driver's license if one was lost or stolen. Notify the Bureau of Motor Vehicles and obtain a new one with a new number rather than a duplicate copy of the old one.
- Change locks if keys were lost or stolen.
- Call other card issuers to report the loss or theft of library cards, movie rental cards, gym membership cards, health insurance cards, and other types of membership cards. Notify any business or organization in which one has a membership that extends credit or permits the use of a private facility.
- Call a lawyer. Whether or not an identity theft victim will require legal services to recover their identity depends on the type and extent of the damage they have experienced, but it's good to consult a lawyer early in the process.

SUMMARY

According to Jonathan Citrin, "When it comes to identity theft, the ideal situation is to prevent it." If prevention does not succeed in staving off the thieves, then the next best thing is to be quick about finding out when an identity has been stolen and is being used fraudulently.[13]

According to the Office of the Victim Advocate of Connecticut, "Today, identity theft is a part of life." If it is not a personal experience, it has happened to someone known to a friend or family member. Stories about identity theft appear in the news constantly when security breaches happen to companies and organizations that thought they had a secure system for storing people's personal identifying information. It is imperative for people to know how to detect, report, and recover from identity theft if it happens to them.

Identity Theft
on the Internet

According to a Web site that offers recommendations on how to pro-
tect against identity theft and fraud, 19-year-old Ken was satisfied
with his computer. A young art history student, he used his computer
regularly. He had e-mail, access to the Internet for research, some
software that he used for school projects, a scanner, and a few games.
It never occurred to Ken to add extra software to make his computer
more secure. That is, not until he learned that his computer had been
breached. But by then, it was too late.

Ken hadn't thought of himself as a very viable target for an
identity thief; as a student, he didn't have many assets for someone
to take. And, he didn't really consider himself to be very vulnerable,
because his Internet usage was limited primarily to academia. So,
it was with great shock that he learned that his computer had been
hacked and that someone had established a whole separate (not so
nice) version of himself.

He found out when one of his fellow students approached him,
and then asked when he had gotten out of jail. The student said he

had read in the weekend paper about Ken's arrest for methamphet-amine trafficking. Ken knew there was a mistake, but after the third person made a comment about the story, Ken thought he had better check with the police to find out what was going on.

It turned out that the man they had arrested (long since released on bail) was Ken in every legal respect. He had used Ken's driver's license as identification when he was arrested. His home had yielded credit cards and doctor bills in Ken's name. Once the police knew that the man had been an imposter, it seemed unlikely that he would return for his court appearance.

When the case was investigated, police learned that the drug trafficker had hacked into someone else's PC and found Ken in the address book there. He then hacked into Ken's computer and there he hit the jackpot! He found the file where Ken stored his scanned images of all of his important documentation—a file he had created prior to copying it to a CD for storage in a safe deposit box. Ken had not deleted the file. Now he truly wishes he had taken the trouble to protect his computer.[1]

The Internet is an engineering marvel consisting of computers, communication software and hardware, and protocols that allow the digital exchange of information between computers. An individual with a personal computer needs only to hire an Internet Service Provider (ISP), which is a private business that will, for a fee, connect their customers to the Internet.[2]

According to the editors of *Kiplinger*, a Washington, D.C.-based publisher of business forecasts and personal finance advice, "Out there on the Internet, there is information about virtually everyone, because from the time a person is born, that individual begins acquiring records about their existence." Some of the records are public. Some are for the purposes of wages and taxation. Some records track financial histories for the purpose of determining credit worthiness.[3]

An incredible amount of information about people is available on the Internet in public records, which are created whenever people interact with the legal system or the government. Births, deaths, marriages, divorces, and a host of other events are a matter of public record. Records about the events in people's lives have been main-tained for longer than people have been able to put pen to paper.[4]

To take advantage of the system, people can run a background check on themselves. It may seem silly, but if an identity has been stolen, it could have been used as identification in an arrest.

Another thing people can do is to be mindful of their presence on the Internet. Are they leaving an identification trail? Shopping is just one Internet activity that might provide an identity thief with lucrative information. Be sure when shopping electronically, that the Web site is considered secure. It should say on the Web site that it is secure; another sign is the "s" in the URL after http: https.[5]

GATHERING INFORMATION ON THE INTERNET

The theft of an individual's identity alone is not much of a crime. It is only when that information is used to commit fraud that an actual crime takes place. Having the victim's identity makes it possible to steal from that person by deceiving others into believing that the thief is that person. The thief is given access to what is rightfully the property of the victim. However, the attempt to get the information in the first place is not fraud. It is not even illegal in and of itself. Some methods of stealing identities from people are so popular (meaning that identity thieves commonly use them), that the tech-niques have their own names: phishing and pharming.

Phishing

Hang out the sign: "Gone Fishing." Go down to the creek with a pole, a hook, and some fancy lures, and catch some dinner. *Phish-ing*, however, means going down to the Internet, casting out some cool lures—and catching dinner too! Or, at least, it is catching the personal identifying information that can be used to buy dinner. The hacker uses bait in the form of e-mails that will hook the victim by getting him to go to the hacker's Web site. Once there, the hacker gathers the information the victim willingly offers. But then, the hacker may slip some software onto the naïve victim's computer, where it will gather a lot more information than the victim willingly provided in responding to the phony e-mail.

Damages from Phishing Attacks

Phishing, as a form of identity theft, has become quite popular with identity thieves. The relative ease of tricking victims into thinking it is safe to enter personal identifying information into a form online makes it a lucrative, if not illegal, business. The damages of a successful phishing attack can be disastrous. The identity thief can use the personal identifying information to commit fraud in the form of

IDENTITY THEFT
IN SOCIAL NETWORKS

According to IdentitySupport.com (which offers identity theft protection services), "The hot new trend of the 21st century is an Internet phenomenon known as social networking." Facebook and Twitter are a few of the better known social networking sites that allow people (often with similar interests) to develop and maintain Internet relationships. These networks, like the Internet itself, can be tremendously powerful tools for creating and strengthening relationships between people, as was seen in the spring of 2011, during the social revolutions in Egypt, Libya, Yemen, Syria, and other countries around the Middle East, which was sparked at least in part by communications made via Facebook and Twitter.[6]

The Web security firm Webroot has reported that about one-third of social network users have enough personal information visible in their profiles to make them vulnerable to identity theft. Family connections, birthdays, addresses, phone numbers, and even pets' names can all be clues for identity thieves. Users who make such information public are making it easy for criminals to take advantage of them.[7]

account takeover or account creation. The thief might have enough information to drain a bank account. Or, a thief might sell the identity to an individual who needs a fresh start or an identity to use in getting a job.[8]

Anti-Phishing

Safe computing practices are needed to prevent identity theft through phishing. Phishing is a combination of technological deception and a ploy known as social engineering. This means tricking people into revealing information that they would not normally reveal. Phishing e-mails often resemble those from legitimate companies or services. Often they include language to shock the recipient, such as saying that their bank account will be frozen if they do not respond. Phishing relies on the victim to go along with the scam and on technology to reach the victim. Prevention needs to address both components.

Many phishing scams require that the hacker make replicas or clones of a business Web site, even duplicating some of the Web site's functions to make it look real. There are now companies that provide a service to the owners of e-business Web sites that consider themselves likely to be victims of phishing scams. The companies offer to eliminate phishing threats by monitoring and detecting phishing incidents; and, they pursue incidents through takedown and resolution.[9]

The federal government has twice considered legislation against phishing, but no law has yet been passed. The first bill was the Anti-Phishing Act of 2005. The second was the Anti-Phishing Consumer Protection Act of 2008. The latter would have prohibited the collection of identifying information of individuals by false, fraudulent, or deceptive means through the Internet, and it would have provided the Federal Trade Commission the necessary authority to enforce such prohibition. Nevertheless, every state in the union has at least one anti-phishing law on its books.[10]

The Anti-Phishing Working Group is an industry association formed to combat phishing. The group's goal is to eliminate the risk of fraud and identity theft from phishing and similar scams, such as spoofing. The APWG educates the public about the risks of phishing, takes reports of phishing, tracks phishing activity, and keeps statistics about phishing. The APWG Public Education Initiative organizes and supports efforts to fight online crime. More information is available at http://www.antiphishing.org.

Pharming

Pharming is a scam in which someone hijacks a legitimate Web site and redirects its visitors to the hacker's illicit Web site. In businesses and organizations, security falls first into the hands of information technology (IT) personnel and their staffs. These are the individuals who use their technological skills to install and manage security hardware and software. The security hardware and software is designed to prevent hackers from getting access to hardware and software like domain name system (DNS) servers, which are used in pharming, databases (used to store information), and Web site page software (used in phishing). Security exists so that the holes in these systems do not give hackers the opening that they need to steal through techniques such as pharming. Yet, as fast as IT professionals devise new methods to keep hackers out, the hackers come up with new ways to get in. At this point there is no definitive solution.[11]

Pharming Techniques Used to Steal Identities

Identity thieves use pharming to deceive victims into handing over their account numbers and passwords, tricking them into thinking that they are giving it to their bank, credit card provider, or other financial service institution. First the hacker creates an exact duplicate of a Web site. Then he or she hacks into a DNS server and reroutes the victim to the duplicate Web site. Or, the hacker gets access to a person's computer and modifies the host's file. DNS servers and host files are used to direct a user to the Web site they name in the URL. When the victim, who believes that the Web site is the actual Web destination he is seeking, enters his account information into the Web site, the hacker has what she wants.[12]

TYPES OF ASSOCIATED INTERNET CRIMES

Several types of crimes are associated with Internet identity theft. The following are some of the more common ones:

- new account creation
- account takeover
- fraudulent transactions[13]

Creating New Accounts

An identity thief who steals enough of a person's information can open new credit accounts with it as though they were that person. The identity thief can use this new line of credit to acquire expensive items that can be resold or request cash advances. Then the identity thief leaves the unpaid account for the victim to deal with. Identity thieves get the information they need to open new accounts from a variety of sources, including accessing public records, hacking into online accounts, or gathering personal data from social networking sites.[14]

Taking Over Existing Accounts

Making purchases on someone else's credit account with a stolen identity is known as account takeover. The thief steals personal identifying information and uses it to purchase items on their victim's account, to get cash advances, or to open additional accounts. The thief may obtain a person's account information in many ways:

- using chat room information
- site cloning (pharming)
- false merchant site
- cracking and hacking[15]

Using Chat Room Information

Identity thieves may visit chat rooms to pick up a visitor's Internet Protocol (IP) address, which they can then use to hack into the visitor's unprotected computer at their leisure.[16]

Site Cloning

Having an identity stolen from a cloned e-commerce site adds insult to injury for the unsuspecting shopper, who logs on to the site not realizing that it is only a copy of the Web site they wanted. Sometimes the whole Web site has been cloned, so the victim does all of his shopping on the cloned site. This is similar to pharming.[17]

False Merchant Sites

A false merchant site is one that advertises prices for the same goods as other e-commerce sites do. And, if the false merchant site were legitimate, their prices would be a great bargain! The trick is that these sites require customers to provide their credit card information before actually shopping on the site.[18] Of course, any orders that customers place will never be filled, but the identity thief will have their credit card information.

Cracking And Hacking

Hacking and cracking are terms that are used somewhat interchangeably in the media; however, hackers typically are individuals who are very good with technology and use their skills to gain access to computer systems that are considered secure, but not necessarily with malicious intent. Crackers, on the other hand, are hackers with malicious intent; their reason for cracking into secure systems is to steal.[19] A hacker can get information about accounts by hacking directly into a company's databases.

Fraudulent Transactions

In a fraudulent transaction, one of the parties involved is not who they represent themselves to be or is using unauthorized information to complete the transaction. Often the party committing fraud provides false or illegally obtained information for the purchase of goods or services. Online, this can involve credit card fraud. Identity thieves may steal a person's credit card information and use it to make unauthorized purchases at online merchants. When purchasing goods, the thieves work fast, sometimes choosing express

PASSWORDS

Passwords can be difficult to remember; to make recalling a password easier when jumping from one application or account to another, many people choose one password and use it everywhere. Bad idea. Hackers, who manage to get a victim to choose a password on a cloned site, will try that password first when they hack into the victim's personal computer and try to access his or her accounts. If their victim uses the same password for all of her accounts, the hacker gains instant access to everything in the victim's name.[20]

A strong and unique password should be created for each account. Do not keep it taped to the desk beside the computer. Do not create a file in the computer named "Passwords" and enter that name for all accounts, the member names used, and the passwords to the accounts in it. If a hacker invades the computer, he will have access to that file.[21]

shipping to limit the time a merchant has to detect the fraud before shipping it. Many banks and other financial institutions have safeguards for detecting this type of fraud and will alert their customers to suspicious activity on their account.

SECURING A PERSONAL COMPUTER

The personal computer that an individual uses probably sits in a home or office, seemingly safe and away from the prying eyes of the denizens of the Internet. Or is it? If the computer is ever used to accesses the Internet, then that computer is not isolated.

Getting In: The IP Address and E-Mail

Every device on the Internet has an Internet Protocol address that makes it possible for them to communicate with the other devices on the Internet. Whether it is a static (permanent) address or one assigned from a pool by the Internet Service Provider, it is unique to that device while it is being used on the Internet. The IP address goes out with e-mails people send from that device (like a return address on an envelope). Web sites store information about their visitors,

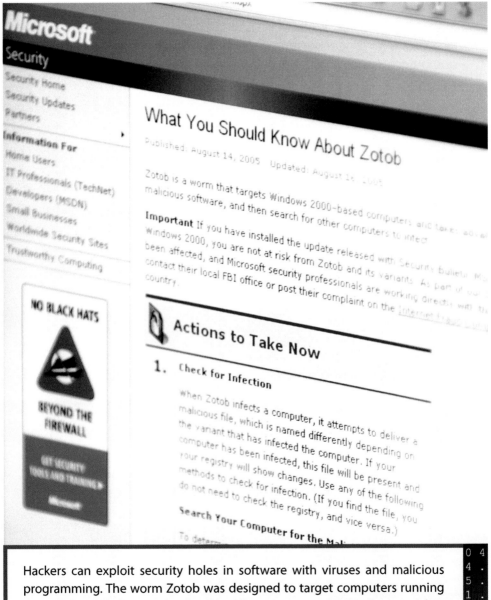

Hackers can exploit security holes in software with viruses and malicious programming. The worm Zotob was designed to target computers running Microsoft Windows 2000 and affected operations at CNN. *(Source: Adam Berry/Bloomberg via Getty Images)*

including IP addresses. It is not something that is kept secret because it is needed for communication. As a result, hackers have learned how to use IP addresses to take advantage of their victims.

The strategy then is to prevent the hacker from getting access to the computer through the IP address and to keep out viruses, spyware (software that transmits user information to another user or company), and all types of malware (software designed to prevent a computer from operating) before they can make the PC vulnerable. When software is developed, there may be security holes that give hackers access to some part of the computer that is running the software. As patches come out with the fix for these security holes, the user must install the patches by updating the software. Sometimes the software does this automatically when users are connected to the Internet, and this effectively closes that particular door to a hacker for the short run. In the long run, keeping up to date with patches and updates to software that is on a computer goes a long way to keeping hackers from getting in. It is also necessary to install and run antivirus software and a firewall.

ANTIVIRUS SOFTWARE

Some hackers write programs that are designed to spread like a virus and are intended to cause chaos and destruction in computers. Programs like these are everywhere, and antivirus software protects computers against them. These programs look at items that come into a computer via e-mail, the Internet, or various forms of digital media to see if they contain a virus. The program has a list of viruses and looks for them when it scans a computer or file. This list should be updated regularly from the Internet so that it is current with the latest threats. The program identifies potential viruses and prevents them from being admitted to the computer.

Another layer of protection comes from having a firewall, which is hardware or software designed to protect a computer from attacks by hackers. Data comes into a computer in small chunks, called "packets." The firewall analyzes each packet, and based on what it finds, it allows the packet to enter the computer or keeps it out. The firewall stands guard, letting in or letting out only what the user has told the filters to allow. The level of protection can be adjusted by the user. There are hardware firewalls, and there are firewalls that only require software to do the job.

For example, according to the State of Michigan Department of Technology Management and Budget (DTMB), "Hardware firewalls provide a strong degree of protection from most forms of attack coming from the outside to the internal network. Hardware firewalls can protect computers on a local area network and they can be implemented without much configuration difficulty."[22]

On the other hand, according to the DTMB, "Software firewalls are installed on individual computers and they need sufficient configuration to be effective. Software firewalls contain a set of related programs, usually located at a network gateway server, that protect the resources of a private network from users on other networks or from internal users. Software firewalls allow application screening to verify the interaction between the requesting client and the requested resource."[23]

SUMMARY

The Internet is very young and very vulnerable. According to Software and Information Industry Association, "What began in the 1960s as a tiny computer network with a few private users was only the embryo of the baby Internet that was born into the public in the late 1980s and 1990s." The Internet is still maturing. For the time being, as wonderful as it is, it cannot be considered safe. People must go "out there" to take advantage of the many benefits the Internet offers: almost instant access to information, a shopping bazaar beyond belief, and the ability to communicate with people around the world, to name but a few. But to go "out there" is to risk becoming a victim of identity theft. Knowing about the cons and scams, the phishing and pharming, the tricks and hacking, is the first step. Being aware of the methods that identity thieves and hackers are using to target victims is the best preventative form of protection. One should also make sure to use technology, such as antivirus software, to protect the hardware and software used to access the Internet. Minimizing the risk of identity theft online is about making it difficult for hackers and identity thieves to acquire personal information.[24]

Protecting Identity Information

About a year after Kathy opened her first checking account, she received an astonishing call from her bank. Someone in Europe had used her debit card. The bank contacted Kathy because foreign transactions were not allowed on the type of account she had opened. If it hadn't been for the restriction on foreign transactions, the identity thief may have gone on using Kathy's debit card and cleaned out her bank account. That is probably what would have happened, if Kathy had any money in her account to steal. Being a young student with little cash turned out to be a form of protection against debit fraud card. People can't steal what isn't there.

Kathy was very angry to learn that someone had a copy of her debit card. It meant that the identity thief had to have her PIN as well. How could this have happened, she wondered? The bank explained to Kathy that debit card fraud is becoming a fairly common form of identity theft. Identity thieves use machines that record the information on a debit card. All they must do is swipe the *victim's card in the card cloning device, something they can do quickly while the victim's attention is elsewhere. If the identity thief watches closely while the victim entered her PIN number at an ATM, he is then able to use the cloned card with the victim's PIN to take out any available cash.*

Kathy now thinks that her experience was a good thing, since she actually lost nothing and learned a great deal. She is very careful these days when she uses her new debit card. Kathy does not let a server or a clerk take it out of her sight. She also shields the key pad with one hand while she enters her PIN with the other. And, thanks to Kathy having little money in her bank account at the time of her attack, she learned another trick. Kathy keeps most of her money in her savings account—one that has no debit card associated with it. She keeps only enough for small, routine purchases in her checking account most of the time. When Kathy wants to use her debit card to pay bills or make a larger purchase, she transfers enough money from her savings account to cover the expense. Internet banking— something else Kathy is very careful with—makes it possible to transfer money conveniently at short notice.[1,2]

Teenagers and children have identities that are ripe for the picking for several reasons. First, a teenager's credit is usually virginal: It has been unused thus far in the teen's life, and consequently the credit report is unblemished by negative marks of any kind. What more could an identity thief want? With the teen's name and Social Security number, new accounts can be created and used with impunity. It is unlikely that the teen has begun to check the credit report yet, so detection is not likely, at least for a while. This gives identity thieves plenty of time to defraud the new accounts. An identity thief can clone the teen's identity for their own use, or to sell it on the black market. There are people who cannot use their own identity to conduct everyday affairs because their credit is damaged or they are not legal citizens of the United States or for other reasons. Buying the identity of a young person means they have a longer period of time to be "safe" with the stolen identity.

THE INTERNET ITSELF

According to Steven Dowshen, M.D., "The Internet is a whole new world, a place of entertainment, research, communication, and social networking." Once a person begins to function "out there" on the Internet, they develop a persona that may be different than the one they actually have in person. This is especially true when someone joins a social networking site, where there is a measure of anonymity that allows a person to try out a facet of their personality that they have not developed yet. When the person logs on to a social networking site, they choose a screen name. As they use instant messaging or post blogs, they begin to grow an online identity, which may or may not be similar to their real identity.[3]

TEEN IDENTITY THEFT PROTECTION, IMPLEMENTATION, AND DEPLOYMENT

In the everyday world, people come to know other people by the way they look and the way they behave. Are they polite and thoughtful in the way they treat people? Are they bad tempered and abusive? Do they take life seriously and work to get ahead in school? Do they forget to keep promises and lose things all the time? The answers to questions such as these are the things that define people in the eyes of others. One's identity (the combination of one's physical appearance and social behavior) is built up over time, and once people have come to think of others a certain way, it is difficult to change their opinion about those people. The persona a person creates online is very similar to this.

Social Networking

An online identity is real. It may seem like a game to present oneself in a way that would seem "over the limit" in real life. It might seem to someone that people online do not know who they are, that they are anonymous, or that they do not take their behavior online seriously. But the opposite is true. Even people who think they are anonymous online can be identified, and people are paying attention to what others are doing on the Internet. Online actions can have real-world consequences. One's online identity will follow them through their lives, as surely as will one's behavior in the everyday world.[5]

Social networking sites pose a special pitfall for teens. It seems great to be connected so easily and quickly to one's friends and family via sites such as Facebook. It is almost like having friends around all the time. The important difference is that things that are said and done while hanging out with friends in the privacy of one's home may not be appropriate online, where many people can read and see what is posted. Social networking users who get too relaxed online risk giving away sensitive personal information or posting something that will get them in trouble.

Equally important is the fact that nothing posted online is temporary. There are no take-backs online. It is a digital world, so whatever one says or posts online is forever. One may post something, and later, upon second thought, regret the posting and delete it, but posted data can be saved or cached by the social network or other outside sites. Embarrassing online posts can haunt someone for years. Worse, if someone posts personal data online, they are only making it easy for identity thieves to target them.

Mark Profiles as Private

When joining Facebook, MySpace, or similar social networking sites, people should realize that much of the information that is given out, either in profiles, account information, or posts, is available to the world. There are some precautions that people can and should take to protect themselves. Read the privacy policy and safety tips provided by social networking sites. Take safety seriously. People should keep their profile marked as private, so that only friends can see their personal information.[6]

For example, according to Facebook, "Both adults and minors have some basic information (name, profile picture, gender, and networks) appear when people navigate to their profile. This information may be accessed by applications that they and their friends use. Adults and minors both appear in search results on Facebook.

Members of Facebook, MySpace, and other social networking services are often lax about privacy and security. Private information, such as phone numbers or e-mail addresses, posted on these Web sites can be used to steal a person's identity. *(Source: AP Photo/The Canadian Press, Sean Kilpatrick)*

However, minors do not have public search listings created for them."[7]

Furthermore, according to Facebook, "The 'Everyone' setting works differently for minors than it does for adults. When minors set information like photos or status updates to be visible to 'Everyone,' that information is actually only visible to their friends, friends of friends, and people in any verified school or work networks they have joined. The only exceptions are for 'Search for me on Facebook' and 'Send me friend requests,' where if the minor has set those to 'Everyone,' the 'Everyone' setting is respected by all."[8]

Stay Up To Date

When one changes an e-mail address, it is important to update any online profiles connected to that address. Online servers use e-mail addresses to identify users. It is access to the e-mail address that enables users to log on to services in order to edit profiles and reset passwords. If one is considering getting rid of an old e-mail address, be sure to visit any online profiles that must be canceled or deleted before making the actual change.[9]

Do Not Respond to Inappropriate Requests

It does not hurt to ask, right? That certainly seems to be the philosophy of predators and identity thieves. Many teens receive requests for personal information from total strangers, and some even give out their information. People do not have the right to personal information or to pictures or to have a meeting just because they ask for it. The safest course of action when someone makes an inappropriate request is to ignore it. If the request makes a person uncomfortable or frightened, talking it over with a parent or a trusted adult is advisable.[10]

AVOIDING SOCIAL ENGINEERING TRAPS: THE NIGERIAN E-MAIL SCAM

Here's a news flash: That Nigerian prince who sent the e-mail requesting help to get millions of dollars of inheritance money he

SAFEGUARD PASSWORDS AND CHANGE THEM FREQUENTLY

Jan's ex-boyfriend, who was feeling angry and rejected by Jan, knew her online passwords. To get back at her for dumping him, he logged on as her and started advocating the legalization of drugs via her pages on MySpace and Facebook. All of Jan's friends and family, who were connected to her through these sites, saw the posts. Many of them were outraged or disappointed, and some posted mean comments in reply. By the time Jan figured out what had happened and changed her password, a lot of damage had been done to her reputation.

Such things happen all too frequently. Making sure that passwords are not easily accessible (like posted on the side of the computer monitor) or simple (like a pet's name) is important to prevent the possibility of someone with a grudge getting to it, or worse, giving it to an identity thief. The best friend of today could be the worst enemy of tomorrow. Make a password strong by using random numbers and letters. At the very least, use two words with numbers either sandwiched in between or at the beginning or end. Make it as hard as possible for someone to guess.[11]

is due—and will share in exchange for the help he needs—is really a con artist. Who knew? Fortunately, most people do these days but not everyone. According to the Web site Hoax-Slayer.com, "The scam is actually very old, but it works—to the tune of over $5 billion in estimated losses in the United States." The scam is also known as the 419 Fraud, named after a section of the Criminal Code of Nigeria. Prior to the arrival of the Internet and e-mail, the scammers used snail mail and other means to reach out to potential victims. The scam has been so successful that it has many imitators with many versions of the stories. It is a classic example of a social engineering scam.[12]

The Nigerian scam may seem funny. How silly to think that a Nigerian prince has one's e-mail! In fact, actress Anne Hathaway (*The Devil Wears Prada*) poked fun at the scam in the October 4, 2008, episode of *Saturday Night Live*, when she said in her opening monologue that her new boyfriend was a Nigerian prince. But, for those who have fallen victim to the scam, there is nothing funny about it.[13]

In response to the infamous Nigerian e-mail scam, the Nigerian government has launched a campaign to crack down on such activity. Notices posted in Internet cafes warn users against engaging in fraudulent e-mail campaigns. (*Source: AP Photo/Sunday Alamba*)

HOW NIGERIAN SCAMS WORK

The scam works like this: A letter or e-mail arrives and it is supposedly from a person who needs help. The person may claim to be a
Nigerian prince or the widow of a wealthy man or any number of
other characters with any nationality. He is contacting the recipient
because there is a large sum of money (an inheritance, government
funds, money for charity, and so on) that he needs to move to a safe
place. If the person who receives the e-mail is willing to help, that
person will be allowed to keep a certain percentage of the money for
himself. The person can help by sending the fees required to move
the money. The fees may be for taxes, bribes, or other necessities.[14]

If a person falls for the scam and sends the advance fees
requested, there will be more advance fees needed soon, and then
more. The requests for more money will only stop when the person realizes she is being scammed and stops sending money. By
that time, it may be that the con man behind the scam has enough
information about the victim to take money directly from her bank
account or to clone the victim's identity.[15]

WHAT TO DO IF A NIGERIAN SCAM
MESSAGE IS RECEIVED

Do not reply!!! The people that send out these scams are real
criminals and they really hurt people. It might seem interesting to
respond to a scammer to see how far he will take the con, but do not
be fooled. Aside from the financial loss, the 419 scams have been
associated with serious crimes like kidnapping and murder. Once
the scammer has a specific person's e-mail address, the scam may
turn into a real threat. Instead, contact your local U.S. Secret Service
office and inform them of the situation.[16]

WHAT TO DO IF INFORMATION OR MONEY HAS BEEN
SUBMITTED TO NIGERIAN SCAMMERS

The 419 (Nigerian) scammers often ask for different types of personal
identifying information as part of a scam. If a victim has already sup-
plied information (banking details or copies of personal documents)
and then realizes that the solicitation is a scam, the victim will send

no more money or information. Yet, when scammers realize that their victim has cut them off, they are likely to take other action—they may steal the victim's identity and wipe out accounts to the best of their ability. One should immediately take action to prevent or minimize identity theft by notifying banks or credit card issuers and closing or changing accounts. If one has already provided the 419 scammers with advance fees, the chances are slim that any money may be recovered.

The best steps to take at this point are to report the scam to the U.S. Secret Service at the fax number below, or make a report by e-mail to 419.fcd@usss.treas.gov. Also submit hard copies of all e-mails and other documentation by U.S. Mail to:

U.S. Secret Service
Financial Crimes Division
950 H Street, NW
Washington, D.C. 20001
(201) 406-5031

Here again, the victim should take all appropriate action to prevent or minimize identity theft.[17]

SAFEGUARDING IDENTITY INFORMATION: SHRED IT!

According to About.com, "Because young children and teenagers are in danger of becoming victims of identity theft, it is important for them to learn good self-protection habits as early in life as possible."[18] Just as young people learned at an early age not to speak to strangers, they need to learn about the risks of having their identity stolen. The responsibility for protecting the young from identity thieves does not rest only with educators and parents. There are many steps that teens can and should take for themselves:

- Do not give out personal or family information to new acquaintances. Chatting with someone in a casual way may seem fun and harmless, and so it is, if the young person is conscious of keeping private information private.

- Stay aware of personal conduct on the Internet and develop the discipline required to think before posting, texting, blogging, or IMing. Be aware of information that should not be posted online: bank account information, credit card numbers, Social Security number, and so on. Remember that what goes "out there" will probably be "out there" for years in the future.

- Get in the habit of shredding any documents with identifying information, such as credit card statements or offers to open new accounts, before discarding them in the trash.

OTHER EXAMPLES OF SOCIAL ENGINEERING IN IDENTITY THEFT

Those Nigerian princes established such a successful scam that identity thieves all over the world are using it as a model with which to develop their own elaborate cons. These newer versions of the 419s are quite ingenious, hitting victims where they are most vulnerable and capitalizing on legitimate human compassion.

- *Give Till It Hurts:* Requests for charitable donations may seem well intentioned, but if such an e-mail includes a link to a Web site where people can donate, it may be a phishing e-mail, pretending to be from a legitimate charitable organization, such as the American Red Cross or the United Way. It works because many people do really want to help out charitable causes. Once they enter their personal information into the Web site form, though, it is in the hands of the identity thieves. To

Young people may not yet have a lot of cards and member-ships, but they often have a credit or debit card on their parents' account for personal expenses.

- Keep any checkbooks and credit or debit cards in a safe place at home if they will not be needed. Only put them in a purse or wallet when they will be used.

- Develop the habit of keeping purses, book bags, wallets, and other personal items under close watch.[19]

- Question the use of your personal information. If a busi-ness or anyone else requests your Social Security number or personal data, ask them why it is needed and how it will

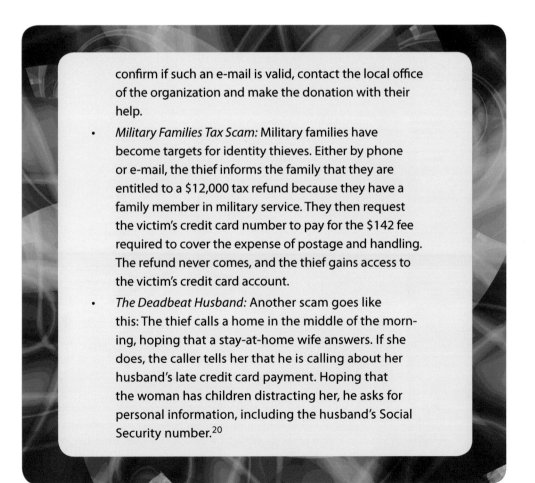

confirm if such an e-mail is valid, contact the local office of the organization and make the donation with their help.

- *Military Families Tax Scam:* Military families have become targets for identity thieves. Either by phone or e-mail, the thief informs the family that they are entitled to a $12,000 tax refund because they have a family member in military service. They then request the victim's credit card number to pay for the $142 fee required to cover the expense of postage and handling. The refund never comes, and the thief gains access to the victim's credit card account.

- *The Deadbeat Husband:* Another scam goes like this: The thief calls a home in the middle of the morn-ing, hoping that a stay-at-home wife answers. If she does, the caller tells her that he is calling about her husband's late credit card payment. Hoping that the woman has children distracting her, he asks for personal information, including the husband's Social Security number.[20]

be used. If they do not give a specific, legitimate reason, then politely decline to give it out. Just because it is "on the form" is not a good enough reason.

TECHNOLOGY

Many everyday technologies bring a risk of identity theft, and identity thieves make full use of technology to steal personal information. There are crackers who get unauthorized access to secure data. There are credit card swiping machines. There are

One way of preventing identity theft is to safeguard any information or documents you may have at home. Government-issued documents such as a birth certificate, Social Security card, or a passport should be kept in a safe place. *(Source: PRNewsFoto/Sentry®Safe)*

malware attacks on personal computers. There are methods of getting access to unprotected wireless networks. These are just a few examples of the ways identity thieves use technology to rob individuals of their identities. Technology can also be used to combat these activities.

Software and Hardware

According to eHow.com, "Because of the huge losses of money to identity thieves, businesses have invested a lot of money in developing technology that helps fight identity theft." Businesses have also invested a lot of revenue in safeguarding people's stored personal information. There are antivirus and anti-spyware programs available that can detect malware, such as viruses and Trojan horses. Ad-Aware and Spybot are two examples of popular antivirus and anti-spyware software.[21] Other programs include McAfee Internet Security and Norton Antivirus, but there are many other similar products available.

Although IT and security professionals are trying to keep up with the new threats, hackers and crackers are faster in coming up with new programs (malware) designed to wreak havoc in the world of cyberspace. One of the purposes of malware is to allow a hacker to steal login IDs and passwords to accounts, as well as any financial information like credit card numbers and bank account information. User can also purchase special electronic hardware that can help protect data. This kind of hardware works by recognizing attempts at theft, and when it finds them, it blocks the intruder from gaining access to the data.[22]

Biometrics

Physical security is critical when it comes to protecting data. One facet of physical security is the use of biometrics to restrict access. There are many biometric security systems that can scan an individual's physical characteristics such as fingerprints, retina patterns, or voiceprints. These data are then stored in a system and must be matched by the original (the individual they came from) in order for access to be granted.[23] Many laptops now include a fingerprint scanner, which users can set up to recognize their print. To log on to the machine, they swipe their finger over the scanner.

Monitoring Systems

Banks and credit card providers have a lot to lose because of identity theft, so they use a variety of methods to prevent it, and to detect it while it is happening. Monitoring systems may be used to identify transactions that appear to be suspicious. If a suspicious transaction appears (for example, a credit card is used for a purchase in Spain when the owner lives in Omaha), the credit card company may contact the card holder to be sure that the transaction is legitimate. If the card owner is not in Spain and has no idea why her card is being used there, action can be taken to track the identity thief and stop the fraud before it does too much damage.[24]

SUMMARY

Identity theft is a serious crime that impacts millions of individuals each year. The protection of personal identifying information, such as an individual's Social Security number, name, and date of birth, can help prevent identity theft. Identity theft occurs when such information is used without authorization to commit fraud or other crimes. While progress has been made to protect personal identifying information in the public and private sectors, challenges remain on how to combat identity theft. Three major challenges are:

- the problem of identity theft itself
- getting the federal, state, and local governments to take steps to prevent potential identity theft
- vulnerabilities that remain in protecting personal identifying information in federal information systems

To address these challenges, this chapter has relied primarily on information from individual reports, testimonies, and realistic case studies that raise awareness about public and private sector use of personal identifying information. Federal, state, and local efforts also protect the security of such information to resolve prior significant information-control deficiencies and information-security program shortfalls. The effective implementation of these recommendations by all individuals to protect information and prevent identity theft will continue to strengthen the security posture of the public and private sectors.

Future Solutions
and Technologies

Dmitri Naskovetz thought he had a great idea—one that would make him a lot of money. In June 2007, he decided to make the idea a reality, and arranged with Sergey Semasko to help him set up a Web site called CallService.biz. It was bold! He offered identity thieves a valuable support service.

Naskovetz hired English- and German-speaking people to make phone calls for Russian-speaking identity thieves, so that they could conduct their fraudulent business without raising suspicion. The identity thieves had done all the preliminary work. They had the names, numbers, and information needed to commit the fraud, but, they had to get around the antifraud measures that banks and credit card companies use to spot fraud.

Naskovetz and Semasko promoted their service on another Web site, CardingWorld.cc, advertising that they had already made more than 5,400 of these calls for other clients. The identity thief would provide the necessary information to CallService.biz, pay a fee, and a person fitting the profile of the victim would be selected to make the call.

Naskovetz and Semasko were arrested on April 15, 2010, by the Czech Republic at the request of the United States, and then extradited to the United States. They pled guilty to the charges of conspiracy to commit wire fraud and conspiracy to commit credit card fraud. PCWorld *magazine estimates that Naskovetz and Semasko could face as much as thirty-seven and a half years in prison.*[1]

Maybe Naskovetz would not have had a market for phony callers if identity theft was not so prevalent worldwide. So, how does the world go about making people's identities secure enough that thieves cannot get them in the first place?

There are technologies and practices available today that can go a long way toward making identities more secure, and more are being developed as the Internet evolves. The use of biometrics, digital signatures, and encryption have all found a place in the war to protect privacy and security, and while this technology comes of age and gains acceptance in society, other new methods are being developed every year.

BIOMETRICS

Bio means life in Greek. *Metric* is measurement in Greek. Biometrics means the measurement of life or of a living thing's characteristics. Use of biometrics, at least in the form of fingerprints as an identification method, has been around for quite a long time, especially in law enforcement. Everyone's fingerprints are unique, making them an excellent tool for identification. Relative to the computer industry, biometrics refers to the practice of using people's unique biological qualities to identify them as a particular person. There are many types of biometric identifiers that are presently in use, or in development.[2]

For example, today's schools use biometrics. According to identiMetrics, Inc., a company that provides finger-scanning identification solutions for schools, "Biometrics are used by schools to save time and money, and improve operations. Biometric technology can also provide benefits in terms of convenience, safety, and security. A

USING SOUND AMPLIFIERS TO STEAL IDENTITIES

There are sound amplifiers that are smaller than the palm of a person's hand but powerful enough to allow that person to discreetly listen in on a personal conversation across a room or outside of a financial institution or any other building. Some sound amplifiers will allow an identity thief to hear and record personal conversations from a distance and not get caught. They sit outside of financial institutions so they can gather personal account information.

This type of sound amplification technology has been rapidly evolving since it was used at listening posts during the Vietnam War in the late 1960s, and multiple versions have been rapidly introduced in the market.

Spy recorders take on a myriad of forms; they can be fitted into stuffed teddy bears, watches, pens, and so on. If an identity thief wants an even more discreet recorder for stealing, there are wireless devices that connect them to the victim's personal computer via a USB. Some devices feature an ultrasensitive microphone that captures any sound within its perimeter and transmits it into a receiver. These devices keep on transmitting until the computer is turned off.

Other extraordinarily powerful, electronic listening devices let the identity thief hear and see a conversation from more than 300 feet away. Some have a 20x prism optical system that lets the identity thief zoom in and see up close what he is hearing.

typical first installation in a school is in the cafeteria, where accurate records are critical for reimbursement from the federal government's $12 billion free and reduced lunch program."[3] Schools can then use the same biometric database to identify students to other applications such as those used for attendance, in the nurse's office, in the library or media center, and on the bus. Once biometrics is being used successfully in one part of a school, the idea is usually embraced in other areas as well. Schools even use it for student identification at athletic events and dances to keep out other students who do not belong.[4]

Another implementation of biometrics might include wireless applications that are now being developed to assist large schools in hallway monitoring. This technology can also be applied to off-site student identification for field trips and outdoor events. Emergency identification as a result of a fire or other disaster is a critical use of this technology.[5]

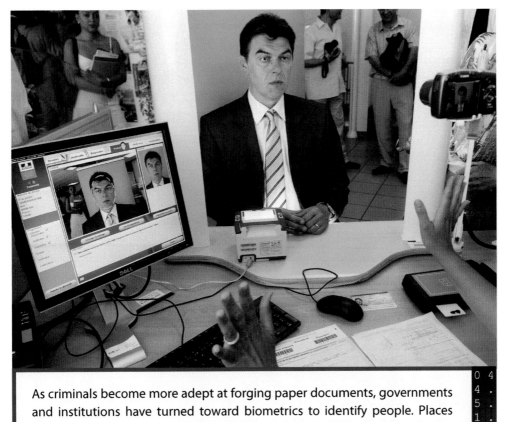

As criminals become more adept at forging paper documents, governments and institutions have turned toward biometrics to identify people. Places such as Marseille, France, can issue passports that include biometric information. *(Source: Sipa via AP Images)*

Furthermore, certain areas in a school should be identified where the use of finger scanning will save that school district time and money, increase productivity, and improve record keeping and, of course, safety.[6]

Finally, the school district should communicate with, educate, and train the people who will be involved in implementing the biometrics technology—whatever it might be. This is usually the weak link in implementing any new type of technology, and implementing biometrics is not much different. The school district will find out that once finger scanning or types of biometrics are being used successfully in one part of the school, the idea migrates and is embraced in other areas as well.[7]

Biometrics Defined

A biometrics-based authentication system is a computer system that measures physical characteristics to identify and authorize its users. These systems are designed to use a variety of individual traits as the identification criteria with only living tissue (not dead, like it is sometimes portrayed in movies): fingerprints, hands, facial scans, retinas, DNA scanning, body, and even odor may be used, and that list is not a bit exhaustive. Behavioral characteristics might include measuring the time elapsed between typing words or gait analysis. These are characteristics that people learn or develop as they live, rather than the characteristics they were born with. Biometrics, like voice identification, may include both physical (pitch and frequencies) and behavioral characteristics, such as dialect and rhythm.[8]

A person who is entitled to have access to a system by virtue of employment, ownership, or for other reasons, may register their biometric data with the system by providing a sample of a characteristic, for example, a fingerprint or a retinal scan. The characteristic is then converted into a digital representation by numerical algorithms. The digital representation, or template, is then entered into the system's database for use in authentication of the user each time access to the system is required.[9]

Biometrics and Identity Theft

According to IdentityTheftFixes.com, "The idea to use biometrics as a means of unquestionable identification for the purposes of getting access to systems or to goods and services, seemed at first to be a method of ending identity theft completely." After all, a credit card number or a PIN can be stolen, but stealing retinal images and fingerprints seemed impossible. However, identity thieves are always only one step behind the developers who implement security technology, ready to find the weak spot. In this case, biometrics data is turned into a string of data, and that data can be stolen the same way credit card numbers can.[10]

When the use of a credit card requires only one form of identification, it is not really a challenge for an identity thief to use it once she has it. This is called "single-factor authentication." Placing an order with a vendor over the telephone often requires nothing more than the credit card number and the expiration date. Even though biometrics is not foolproof, the use of biometrics in a double-factor security solution would be an improvement in protecting personal identification. This method would involve a combination of identification data. It might, for example, use something a person knows, like a PIN or a password, together with a physical item that a person has, like a credit card or a fingerprint.

DIGITAL SIGNATURES

A digital signature provides the user with an individual number that represents the user's legal signature and identity. Think of it like a Social Security number, account number, or a bar code. To sign a document digitally, the user must also use log in accounts to networks and software, which adds on layers of security and identity verification. The digital signature is usually installed on an electronic tape on a card like a hotel key or credit card. When the digital signature is used, it usually requires a PIN to be activated as a legal signature. Therefore every page of a document signed with a digital signature leaves a digital thumbprint as documents are accessed. This is an identity fraud investigator's dream.[11]

Identifying people using biometric data is becoming more prevalent in high-security situations. Many corporations and government facilities use biometric scanners to provide additional security. *(AP Photo/Ric Feld)*

The disadvantage of digital signatures is that in order for them to work, they require technology support and staff, production of card keys, and the hardware to burn the binary code to the electronic tape. If a person loses the card, she cannot sign digitally until a new card is issued. The advantages are that it is the most secure identity theft protection available. An identity thief would have to utilize a host of technologies and electronic intrusion hardware and systems in order to commit fraud using a digital signature. Even if a thief accessed documents already digitally signed, and then copied and pasted a digital signature and placed it on other documents, the date could not be changed. Also, the documents would leave a digital thumbprint that could be traced back to the identity thief.[12]

In other words, a digital signature attached to a document transmitted over a network verifies that the person who sent the document really is who she claims to be. Digital signature technology makes use of something called "public key cryptography." This is a code that locks in an electronic signature, so that it can only be decrypted by someone who knows the key to the code.[13]

A digital signature is equivalent to a person's handwritten signature. The difference between the two is that the digital signature has been encoded, so that the computer can read it. Like a handwritten signature, it can be analyzed to verify that it is a person's authentic signature. This allows users to digitally "sign" a document, and for the document to be guaranteed as unchanged after the person signing it sends it out over the network.[14]

The future of signatures could possibly come in the form of fingerprints or retina scans. For example, recently in Iraq, pictures of people's ears and digital voice capturing were used as a means of identity verification.[15]

How Digital Signatures Work

Digital signatures can help someone who needs to send a sensitive document via the Internet ensure that the recipient receives exactly the same document that is sent. The following steps are needed in order to make that happen:

- A digital certificate must be obtained from a certifying authority. This digital certificate, issued by a trusted third party, verifies that the person using it is who she says she is.
- The sender uses the recipient's public key to encrypt the document before she sends it.
- The recipient then decrypts the document using her own private key.
- The recipient confirms that the document came from the sender and no one else because of the digital certificate attached to it.[16]

The Advantages of Digital Signatures

Secure digital signatures allow business and transactions to occur without having all of the participants together in one place. Other advantages of digital signatures are as follows:

- No longer do parties to a contract need to mail the document back and forth while in negotiation; they can amend the agreement electronically, and when the document is agreed on, it can be signed legally, with a digital signature.
- With digital signatures and digital certificates, there is no risk of imposters and no contract invalidation. In other words, neither party to the contract can claim that someone else impersonated them.
- There is no risk that a document can be tampered with; no party can claim that a document was modified after it left their computer.
- Digital signatures support a green environment by eliminating the need to print documents (they can be stored electronically).
- Off-the-shelf digital signature software and applications make it easy to use digital signature software.[17]

Protect a Digital Signature

There are a multitude of companies offering a variety of software and services to users. Some are willing to give people a free digital signature, some offer software solutions, and many work with specific operating systems and applications. Because a digital signature is legally binding, it is definitely not something one wishes to have stolen. When one attaches a digital signature to a document, it is as if the document had been signed. If the signature has been stolen and used by an identity thief, the victim may have a fight on his hands to prove that the document did not come from him.[18]

ENCRYPTION

Banks and businesses online must ensure that their customers' information is inaccessible to prying eyes. How do they do this?[19] They use encryption. From the time that packet-switched networks came into being in the 1960s, the computer and networking industry, as well as the government, has been working to develop protocols and standards to define the way that computers communicate. The results of that work are the protocols and standards in place that have been implemented so that communication and data transmission is relatively seamless between computers and networks. One of these protocols is a security protocol known as the Secure Sockets Layer (SSL).[20]

In other words, the best way to protect identification information in digital form is to use encryption. SSL and its successor TLS (Transport Layer Security) are examples of technologies used to encrypt data that is transmitted over networks. Encryption should also be used to protect identification information that is stored on disk, tape, CD-ROM, or any other type of media that hold data.

Secure Sockets Layer

Think of a combination lock. An average one might consist of three rings that each run from 0 to 9. A code can be set using any digit between 0 and 9 in the first ring, and the same in the second and third ring. So, a code could be 901 or 019 or any other of the possible combinations using the available numbers. It could take a while,

TRANSPORT LAYER SECURITY

Transport Layer Security is a protocol that ensures privacy between communicating applications and their users on the Internet. When a server and client communicate, TLS ensures that no third party (identity thief) may eavesdrop or tamper with any message.

TLS is composed of two layers: the TLS Record Protocol and the TLS Handshake Protocol. The TLS Record Protocol provides connection security with some encryption method such as the Data Encryption Standard (DES). The TLS Record Protocol can also be used without encryption. The TLS Handshake Protocol allows the server and client to authenticate each other and to negotiate an encryption algorithm and cryptographic keys before data is exchanged.

but eventually, if one tried every possible combination of digits, one could break the code and open the lock.

As packets of data are sent over the Internet, each one is locked using SSL technology. The code to unlock each packet is 128 characters long. What this really means is that it would be almost impossible to get a person's packets of data out of the Internet and virtually impossible to unlock and reassemble those packets of data and turn it into information. Even if that happened, so much time would have passed trying combinations to unlock the code that the data might be useless.[21]

Secure Server IDs (Digital Certificates)

A Secure Server ID, or digital certificate, is issued by a Certification Authority (CA) that allows the CA to vouch for the identity of an online entity. No digital certificate can be issued until the

CA establishes the identity of the entity requesting the digital certificate; but, once they have done this, it can assure others that the entity using the certificate is who it claims to be. The certificate, such as the one issued by VeriSign, allows Web sites to conduct business online with the assurance of data security. A typical Secure Server ID contains the organization's name and physical address, their public key and its expiration data, a unique serial number, and the name of the CA that issued the ID. Online business can advertise that they have been issued a digital certificate as a way of reassuring their customers that their Web site is secure.[22]

Pretty Good Privacy

According to eHow.com, back in 1991, "a fellow by the name of Phillip Zimmerman created the first version of Pretty Good Privacy (PGP), a program for data encryption and decryption." A proposed Senate bill would have required that cryptography programs include a method for the government to decrypt messages, and this prompted Zimmerman to write PGP. Zimmerman and his friends hurriedly distributed PGP to bulletin board systems, so that it would be available to people should the government decide to outlaw cryptography. From there, PGP was distributed worldwide via the Internet. At that time, encryption of more than 40 bits, which PGP provided, was considered to be munitions (or war materiel), so the export of PGP was considered illegal; Zimmerman became the target of a criminal investigation for several years, but he was never charged.[23]

When Zimmerman developed PGP, he combined a public key system (known as RSA) developed by researchers at the Massachusetts Institute of Technology (MIT), and his own symmetric key cipher, which he called Bass-O-Matic. He later replaced Bass-O-Matic with IDEA, which is a more secure symmetric key cipher, to create PGP. However, because RSA was already in use, there were patent ramifications, and Zimmerman was threatened with lawsuits. Eventually Zimmerman agreed to stop distributing PGP, and MIT became the official distributor of PGP.[24]

E-COMMERCE SECURITY

Recent data breaches have brought the issue of identity theft and consumer privacy to the forefront of media attention. In April 2011, the marketing firm Epsilon experienced a data breach. As a marketing firm that sends out about 40 million e-mails a year for its clients, the potential for damages to come from that breach was appalling. Some of Epsilon's clients are major banks and e-commerce sites. Sony experienced three major back-to-back breaches, affecting more than 100 million identities, in April and May 2011. The *E-Commerce Times* reports that "The millions of people whose identities have been compromised must be on guard against fraud on their accounts and phishing attempts, where identity thieves will seek to acquire more information to complete their identities."[25]

Millions of People Exposed

If the recent data breaches have brought the glaring spotlight of media attention to the identity theft problem, they have also generated demands for tougher legislation. There are laws that require companies to notify customers if a data breach might expose the customer to identity theft fraud, but the laws are at the state level. California enacted the first state law that requires companies to notify people in the event of a data breach. The Database Security Breach Notification Act became law in July 2003. Since then, according to the Privacy Rights Clearinghouse, most states have enacted similar legislation. The recent data breaches, however, have turned the focus of the law back to Congress, where representatives from California called for "a uniform national standard for data security and data breach notification."[26]

Companies have been reluctant to offer assistance to victims when there has been a data breach, out of concerns that offering any help may be construed legally as an admission of wrongdoing. All that may change in the near future. On May 12, 2011, the White House sent its Cyber-Security Proposal to Congress. The proposal included the Data Breach Notification Law. Should this proposal pass and become law, specific timelines and specific requirements for notification will be defined at the federal level. Individual states would be able to add additional requirements for companies to follow, when notifying customers of a data breach if they wished. Even so, for companies with a presence in more than one state, the national standard will make life easier.

Legislation Falling Short

E-Commerce Times reports that there is a great push in Congress to address and resolve the problems associated with identity theft fraud. However, there is an aspect of identity theft that may cause any new legislation to be less effective than it should be to really solve the problem."While lawmakers recognize the urgency of addressing the ID theft trend, the laws they are likely to pass will often be softened on their way through the legislative process, thanks to heavy lobbying from corporations, trade groups, and others."[27]

Solving this problem is not in the best interest of lobbyists from businesses and organizations that have an interest in keeping illegal immigrants with stolen Social Security numbers. In other words, the motivation by businesses to hire illegal immigrants with stolen Social Security numbers is to save money. Why should businesses hire American citizens at $15.00 an hour when they can pay an illegal immigrant $7.50 per hour?[28]

Furthermore, a person who does not have a Social Security number may not hold a job in the United States. Illegal immigrants do not have a legal Social Security number because they are not citizens. Also, illegal immigrants may not hold a job in the United States, but they can and do. Illegal immigrants are buying Social Security numbers from identity thieves on the black market.[29]

ILLEGAL IMMIGRATION AND IDENTITY THEFT

One of the areas where serious legal reform is desperately needed is in Social Security number identity theft. This aspect of identity theft is often related to illegal immigration: any noncitizen of the United States must commit identity theft in order to hold a job here. As a result, sales of stolen SSNs are big business. This puts identity theft at the tip of the immigration reform iceberg. Part of the problem is that U.S. government entities, such as the Social Security Administration and the Internal Revenue Service, do not notify people if their SSN is being misused. The same is true of the credit reporting bureaus, which actually put information about the fraudulent use of a person's Social Security number in a subfile under the actual person's name. The actual person may not be able to see the subfile but businesses or other clients may. This practice makes it possible for an identity thief to continue sharing the use of a person's Social Security number, so that they can hold jobs and get credit they are not entitled to.

Employers Fight Changes

According to the Center for Immigration Studies, American businesses, in large part, resist laws that require verification of a potential employee's citizenship status, because verification is not profitable for them.[30] Since the law prohibits the hiring of an individual without a Social Security number, if a company was found to have knowingly hired an illegal alien, it might suffer criminal and financial penalties, not to mention the loss of cheap labor. "Knowingly" is the key word. Verification by using a system like E-Verify would make it impossible to unknowingly hire illegal aliens.[31]

Organizations such as the U.S. Chamber of Commerce and the Associated Builders and Contractors fight to keep verification requirements from becoming law so they can hire illegal immigrants to keep labor costs down.[32] For example, when President George W. Bush issued an executive order that would require federal contractors to use the E-Verify system, human resources associations, along with a vast majority of companies, filed suit to prevent it. Also, chambers of commerce in the states of Arizona and Oklahoma sued to prevent employment verification from becoming law. The goal of this type of lawsuit is to prevent removal of the "knowingly hired" shield that not using E-Verify provides, as well as greed.[33, 34]

SSA and IRS and Identity Thieves

A step in the right direction for fighting identity theft would be if the Social Security Administration accepted responsibility for notifying people when it sees that two or more individuals are using the same Social Security number. They could also notify law enforcement when a SSN that had not been issued shows up in fraudulent use and remove the number from use. Instead, such numbers can still be assigned to an individual through legitimate channels, risking that the person will also become associated with the credit history or any criminal activity already connected to the number.[35, 36]

The IRS could also get involved. When the agency receives a W-2 form with a Social Security number that does not match the individual's name, they generally do not challenge it. Neither does the IRS notify the taxpayer that identity theft is the problem. This happens millions of times a year. If the identity thief who is using the Social Security number under another name fails to pay his or her taxes on money they earned, the real owner of the SSN may be required to pay. If the identity thief files his tax return before the real owner of the SSN does, the real owner may have problems trying to file her own tax return.[37]

Individuals who come to the United States and work here illegally break the law and commit perjury when they use a stolen Social Security number to file federal taxes. There are few deterrents against this because businesses continue to hire them and they receive education, health, and other social benefits from the government. In fact, the situation creates an incentive for illegal immigrants to commit identity theft.[38]

SUMMARY

Technologies and practices exist that can help prevent identity theft. For example, biometrics puts life on the front line as a barrier to technical intrusion into systems. When biometric identification is paired with a pertinent piece of information as a means of gaining access to a system, it is possible to achieve a strong measure of security.

Digital signatures and the use of encryption are highly technical ways to disguise a message as it passes through the networks, and to assure that the recipient of a message has received what the sender actually sent. It also assures the recipient that the sender is actually who he claims to be, because the sender is using a certificate that was issued by a Certification Authority.[39] Yet there are still loopholes and problems in the system that not only allow identity theft to happen but in some ways indirectly encourage it.

Summary, Conclusions, and Recommendations

Elizabeth Esther Reed went to Harvard and to Columbia University. A bright student in high school in Montana, she excelled on her debate team. There was a whole world of wonderful potential ahead of her and she could have done anything. But, when her parents divorced, Esther dropped out of high school. Soon she was stealing. Then, in 1999, she disappeared and her family thought she was dead.[1]

According to CreditIdentitySafe.com (which provides online information and resources to protect individuals from identity theft and fraud), Reed had disappeared, but into another woman's identity. Instead of using all of that great potential to develop a career in something she loved, Reed grew up to be an identity thief. She applied to and was accepted into Harvard as Natalie Bowman, where she joined the debate team. Next Reed took on the identity of Brooke Henson, a woman who had gone missing from South Carolina, and got admitted to Columbia University, where she was an honor student.

When Reed, aka Brooke Henson, applied for a part-time job as a housekeeper, the prospective employer did a background check and saw that she was a missing person. Police questioned Reed, but she told them she really was Henson, but had left a messy domestic abuse situation. When New York police let the South Carolina detective who was working on the missing person case know, he asked for a DNA sample. Police were unable to provide it, because Reed had disappeared.

As Reed's story unraveled, she was profiled on the television program America's Most Wanted *and pursued by the Secret Service and U.S. Marshals. Reed had become quite skilled at obtaining new identity documents from the information she gathered about people. Authorities had questions about Reed being a spy, monies wired from overseas accounts, and claims of being a chess champion, as a front for the money she was using.*

Reed was eventually apprehended in Illinois in 2008, and charged and tried in South Carolina. She pled guilty to fraud and identity theft, and is now serving her four-year prison sentence in the Alderson Federal Prison Camp in West Virginia.[2]

Identity theft really happens. People do become victims of identity theft every day, and the resulting damage to an individual's life and reputation range from the modest and inconvenient, to the very severe. The victim could suffer real losses: loss of money, loss of creditworthiness, loss of opportunities, and loss of reputation. Teens, especially, have a lot at stake when it comes to identity theft. An identity thief can damage a young person's career prospects and their entire future.

TEENS ARE PRIME TARGETS

Most teens (especially ages 13 to 16) do not use their Social Security numbers for employment or to obtain credit; so, parents generally do not check their teen's credit histories, thus allowing an identity thief using a child's SSN to go undetected for years. Sometimes document vendors sell fraudulent identity packages using unassigned SSNs that are later assigned to a teen, causing them problems before they are even born.[3]

For example, "There is a major problem with workers in medical offices stealing teen patients' identities, selling them, and making a direct profit," according to Steven Malanga, senior editor of *City Journal*.[4] The stolen numbers are sold to immigrant smuggling groups (such as coyotes) who use them to fabricate fraudulent documents for people they bring into the United States."[4] "The result of this," according to the *Phoenix Business Journal*, "is that teen identity theft has grown rapidly to an estimated 41.3 million teens having had their identities stolen in 2010."[5]

The FBI reports other examples of teen identity theft such as crime sprees that involve illegal aliens using the SSNs of thousands or more teens. The FBI identified 16,267 companies that were paying wages to the SSNs of teens on public assistance over the age of 13. One teen's SSN was being used by 48 adults. Illegal aliens used those teens' SSNs to get jobs, start businesses, and open bank accounts. One identity thief told FBI agents that he paid $200 for a boy's SSN. Victims included a 15-year-old girl who supposedly traveled 90 miles to her job at a steak restaurant; a 13-year-old boy who apparently owned a cleaning company and worked as a prep cook at three upscale restaurants; and a 14-year-old boy who supposedly worked for an express air freight company. The identity thieves in those cases were charged with third-degree felony counts of identity fraud and forgery.[6]

EMPLOYMENT-RELATED IDENTITY THEFT
According to the FBI, employment-related identity theft is the largest single driver (38 percent) of identity theft. Almost 150 million people became victims of identity theft in 2010. The cost to victims was an estimated $75 billion, with an estimated total of 50.5 million hours dedicated to resolving identity theft issues.[7]

The link between illegal aliens and identity theft has been further confirmed by the Social Security Administration. Real Social Security numbers and accounts are being created, or purloined, by

A policewoman searches a woman outside of a produce processing plant in Oregon. Undocumented workers will often purchase stolen Social Security numbers and green cards to provide to employers. *(Source: AP Photo/Rick Bowmer)*

undocumented workers to circumvent employers' efforts to certify their legality. According to the Social Security Administration, 95 percent of Social Security-related identity theft cases involve people who use their own names, but use someone else's Social Security number. Five percent involve identity thieves using the numbers to assume their victims' identities.[8]

IDENTITY THEFT VICTIMS SUFFER REAL-LIFE CONSEQUENCES

Victims of identity theft suffer real-life consequences. For example, according to the Department of Homeland Security (DHS), "Victims of workers that worked at Swift packing plants in Texas included an individual in Texas whose personal information was being used by an illegal alien for employment. The victim was pulled over and arrested because the illegal alien had used his identity to conduct criminal activity."[9]

In another real-life example, in Illinois, an American citizen was denied a job at a Target store because one of the 37 people who were using her SSN was already employed by the company. According to Technology Correspondent Bob Sullivan of MSNBC, "The woman found herself in a financial nightmare. All those imitators made a mess out of her work history, her Social Security records, and her credit report. She was haunted by bills and creditors. She received threatening letters from the IRS, asking her to pay taxes on money earned by imposters. She was told to repay unemployment benefits she had received, after the government discovered she was 'working' while drawing benefits."[10]

In still another example, reported by the Center for Immigration Studies, "A man whose SSN was used to obtain employment in at least three states was told by the IRS that he owed $64,000 in unpaid taxes in spite of the fact that he had been incarcerated in a state penitentiary during the time the income was earned." Another case "includes an air force veteran who was arrested on a warrant for unpaid parking tickets that were incurred by an illegal alien using his identity. He was only released after paying a $340 fine for tickets that he did not incur. He continued to receive demands for the payment of outstanding taxes on income that he had not earned and he saw his credit rating destroyed."[11]

These cases are only a few examples, but millions of Americans may be sharing their Social Security numbers with illegal aliens. These people may only discover what has happened to them when a bad credit report directly affects their lives when they apply for a loan or receive bills for items they did not purchase. By then, they have a long, hard battle ahead of them to restore their credit and reputation.

INTRODUCTION

1. Federal Trade Commission, "About Identity Theft," Federal Trade Commission, http://www .ftc.gov/bcp/edu/microsites/ idtheft/consumers/about- identity-theft.html#content (Accessed October 19, 2010).
2. Ibid.
3. Jim and Audri Lanford, "ATM Theft: 8 Tips to Protect Yourself from the 5 Most Common ATM Scams," Scambusters.org, http:// www.scambusters.org/atmtheft .html (Accessed February 21, 2011).
4. Federal Trade Commission.
5. Ibid.
6. Ibid.
7. Ibid.
8. Ibid.
9. Ibid.
10. Ibid.
11. Lanford, "ATM Theft."
12. Federal Trade Commission.
13. Ibid.
14. Ibid.
15. Ibid.
16. Ibid.

CHAPTER 1

1. Presentation by the Federal Trade Commission before the Subcommittee on Commerce, Trade, and Consumer Protec- tion of the House Committee on Energy and Commerce, "Identity Theft and Social Se- curity Numbers," Federal Trade Commission, http://www.ftc .gov/os/testimony/040928test .shtm (Posted September 28, 2004).
2. Ibid.
3. Javelin Strategy & Research, "Jav- elin Study Finds Identity Fraud Reached New High in 2009, but Consumers are Fighting Back," Javelin Strategy & Research, https://www.javelinstrategy .com/news/831/92/Javelin- Study-Finds-Identity-Fraud- Reached-New-High-in-2009- but-Consumers-are-Fighting- Back/d,pressRoomDetail (Posted February 10, 2010).
4. Javelin Strategy & Research, "Child Identity Theft Study," Javelin Strategy & Research, http://debix.com/docs/Child_ ID_Theft_Study_2008.10.pdf (Accessed November 14, 2011).
5. ABC News, "Parents Steal Children's Identities," ABC Eyewitness News, http:// abclocal.go.com/wtvd/ story?section=news/ consumer&id=5502284 (Posted July 23, 2007).
6. Identity Theft Resource Center, "ITRC Fact Sheet 120—Identity Theft and Children," Identity Theft Resource Center, http://www.idtheftcenter.org/ artman2/publish/v_fact_sheets/ Fact_Sheet_120_printer.shtml (Posted December 5, 2009).
7. Federal Trade Commission.
8. Matthew Sturdevant, "Travelers Expands Identity-Fraud Coverage," *Hartford Courant*, http://articles.courant .com/2010-11-10/business/ hc-identity-fraud-coverage-

1111-20101110_1_identity-fraud-identity-fraud-travel-expenses (Posted November 10, 2010).

9. Ibid.

CHAPTER 2

1. Identity Theft Resource Center, "ITRC Fact Sheet 120—Identity Theft and Children," Identity Theft Resource Center, http://www.idtheftcenter.org/artman2/publish/v_fact_sheets/Fact_Sheet_120_printer.shtml (Posted December 5, 2009).

2. R. Sinclair, "What Is Financial Identity Theft?" eHow.com, http://www.ehow.com/about_5048320_financial-identity-theft.html (Accessed February 22, 2011).

3. Privacy Rights Clearinghouse/UCAN, "Fact Sheet 17g: Criminal Identity Theft: What to Do if It Happens to You," Privacy Rights Clearinghouse, http://www.privacyrights.org/fs/fs17g-CrimIdTheft.htm (Posted November 2008).

4. Identity Theft Assistance Center, "Case Study: Identity Theft Hits Close to Home in Los Angeles," Identity Theft Assistance Center, http://identitytheftassistance.org/pageview.php?cateid=46 (Accessed February 23, 2011).

5. Ibid.

6. Identity Theft Resource Center.

7. Ibid.

8. Adoption Month, "States That Allow Access To Original Birth Certificates," Adoption.com, http://e-magazine.adoption.com/2010-01/search-reunion (Posted January 2010).

9. Ibid.

10. Identity Theft Assistance Center.

11. Identity Theft Resource Center.

12. John Sileo, "Protect Your Child from the Growing Trend of Identity Theft," Hitched.com, http://www.hitchedmag.com/article.php?id=738 (Accessed April 22, 2010).

13. Ibid.

14. crownofsunbeams (eHow User), "How to Protect Your Children From Identity Theft," eHow Family, http://www.ehow.com/how_2225419_protect-children-identity-theft.html (Accessed April 29, 2011).

15. Enid Edginton, "Types of Identity Theft," EzineArticles.com, http://ezinearticles.com/?Types-of-Identity-Theft&id=491580 (Accessed February 22, 2011).

16. Ibid.

17. Ibid.

18. Ibid.

19. Ibid.

20. Ibid.

CHAPTER 3

1. Halifax, "More Information," Halifax.co.uk, http://www.halifax.co.uk/securityandprivacy/security-centre-home/common-threats/id-theft/?pagetabs=4 (Accessed February 23, 2011).

2. Privacy Rights Clearinghouse/UCAN, "Identity Theft IQ Test," Privacy Rights Clearinghouse, http://www.privacyrights.org/itrc-quiz1.htm (Posted June 2009).

3. Ibid.

4. John Sileo, "Protect Your Child from the Growing Trend of Identity Theft," Hitched.com, http://www.hitchedmag.com/article.php?id=738 (Accessed April 22, 2010).

5. Federal Trade Commission, http://www.ftc.gov/ (Posted May 26, 2010).

6. Vijeta Bhatia, "How to Minimize Identity Theft Risk," EzineArticles.com, http://ezinearticles.com/?How-to-Minimize-Identity-Theft-Risk&id=4110080 (Accessed February 23, 2011).

7. Federal Trade Commission.

CHAPTER 4

1. ID Watchdog, "Consumer Case Studies: Detection: The First Step," ID Watchdog, https://www.idwatchdog.com/casestudy_richard.php (Accessed February 16, 2011).

2. Securian, "Detecting Identity Theft," Securian, http://www.securian.com/Securian/Privacy+policies/Identity+theft/Detecting (Accessed June 16, 2010).

3. Ibid.

4. Jonathan Citrin, "Identity Theft—Early Detection Is Key," CitrinGroup, http://www.citringroup.com/resources/news/news_20050608_01.asp (Posted June 8, 2005).

5. Ibid.

6. Securian, "Detecting."

7. Ibid.

8. Allie Johnson, "Credit Monitoring Services: Pros, Cons, and How to Pick One," Fox Business, http://www.foxbusiness.com/personal-finance/2011/02/23/credit-monitoring-services-pros-cons-pick/ (Accessed July 19, 2011).

9. Privacy Rights Clearinghouse/UCAN, "Fact Sheet 33: Identity Theft Monitoring Services," Privacy Rights Clearinghouse, http://www.privacyrights.org/fs/fs33-creditmonitoring.htm (Posted July 2010).

10. Money-Zine.com, "Reporting Identity Theft," Money-zine.com, http://www.money-zine.com/Financial-Planning/Debt-Consolidation/Reporting-Identity-Theft/ (Accessed June 15, 2010).

11. Ibid.

12. Ibid.

13. Citrin, "Identity Theft."

CHAPTER 5

1. Lynne Conner, "How Computer Hackers Stole My Identity: A Case Study," About Identity Theft, http://www.aboutidentitytheft.co.uk/computer-hackers-stole-identity.html (Accessed July 27, 2010).

2. Tom Arnold, "Internet Identity Theft: 'A Tragedy for Victims,'" Software & Information Industry Association, http://www.authenware.com/presentations/Understanding%20Id%20Theft.pdf (Posted June 2000).

3. *Kiplinger*, "What The Net Knows About You," Yahoo, http://video.search.yahoo.com/search/video?p=the+kiplinger+washington+editors+what+the+net+knows+about+you (Accessed July 25, 2010).

4. Ibid.

5. Ibid.

6. IdentitySupport.com, "Identity Theft in Social Networks," IdentitySupport.com. http://www.identitysupport.com/87-identity-theft-in-social-networks.html (Accessed February 27, 2011).

7. Carrie-Ann Skinner, "Beware: Identity Thieves Harvest Social Networks," *PC World*, http://www.pcworld.com/article/167511/beware_identity_thieves_harvest_social_networks.html (Accessed July 19, 2011).

8. Michigan Department of Technology, Management and Budget, "Social Engineering: Phishing/Pharming," Michigan Department of Technology, Management and Budget, http://michigan.gov/cybersecurity/0,1607,7-217--111902--,00.html (Accessed July 27, 2010).

9. Ibid.

10. Ibid.

11. Ibid.

12. Ibid.

13. Arnold, "Internet Identity Theft."

14. Ibid.

15. Ibid.

16. Ibid.

17. Ibid.

18. Ibid.

19. Ibid.

20. Michigan Department of Technology, Management and Budget, "Social Engineering."

21. Ibid.

22. Michigan Department of Technology, Management and Budget, "Hardware Firewall vs Software Firewall," http://www.michigan.gov/cybersecurity/0,1607,7-217--108698--,00.html (Accessed June 22, 2011).

23. Ibid.

24. Arnold, "Internet Identity Theft."

CHAPTER 6

1. Barbara Correa, "Danger Comes in Numbers with ID Theft Rising, Children Are Most Vulnerable Victims," Los Angeles Daily News, http://www.thefreelibrary.com/DANGER+COMES+IN+NUMBERS+WITH+ID+THEFT+RISING,+CHILDREN+ARE+MOST...-a0146924614 (Accessed July 19, 2011).

2. Sally Aquire, "I Was a Victim of Identity Theft: Case Study," Personal Safety Advice, http://www.personalsafetyadvice.co.uk/being-victim-identity-theft-case-study.html (Accessed March 11, 2011).

3. Steven Dowshen, "Protecting Your Online Identity and Reputation," Kids Health http://kidshealth.org/teen/safety/safebasics/online_id.html (Accessed August 27, 2010).

4. Ibid.

5. Ibid.

6. Ibid.

7. Facebook, "Help Center: Using Facebook Mobile Web," http://www.facebook.com/help.php?page=823 (Accessed June 22, 2011).

8. Ibid.

9. Dowshen, "Protecting."

10. Ibid.
11. Ibid.
12. Brett M.Christensen, "Nigerian Scams—419 Scam Information," Hoax-Slayer, http://www.hoax-slayer.com/nigerian-scams, html (Accessed March 14, 2011).
13. Ibid.
14. Ibid.
15. Ibid.
16. Ibid.
17. Ibid.
18. Jackie Burrell, "5 Ways to Protect Your Teen from Identity Theft, College Identity Theft Protection Tips," About.com, http://youngadults.about.com/od/finances/a/idthefttips.htm (Accessed August 27, 2010).
19. Ibid.
20. Crimes of Persuasion, "Identity Theft Examples Using Social Engineering and Phone Phishing Techniques," http://www.crimes-of-persuasion.com/Crimes/Telemarketing/Inbound/MajorIn/id_theft.htm (Accessed March 14, 2011).
21. Josh Vogt, "Technology Used Against Identity Theft," eHow.com, http://www.ehow.com/about_6301362_technology-used-against-identity-theft.html (Posted April 14, 2010).
22. Ibid.
23. Ibid.
24. Ibid.

CHAPTER 7

1. Robert McMillan, "Belarus Man Pleads Guilty to Running Identity Theft Site," IDG News, http://www.pcworld.com/businesscenter/article/220506/belarus_man_pleads_guilty_to_running_identity_theft_site.html (Posted February 23, 2011).
2. IdentityTheftFixes, "Can Biometrics Prevent Identity Theft?" IdentityTheftFixes.com, http://www.identitytheftfixes.com/can_biometrics_prevent_identity_theft.html (Accessed August 29, 2010).
3. identiMetrics, "Biometric Student Identification: Practical Solutions for Accountability & Security in Schools," identiMetrics.com. http://www.identimetrics.net/articles/Finger-Scanning-White-Paper.pdf (Posted June, 2009).
4. Ibid.
5. Ibid.
6. Ibid.
7. Ibid.
8. Opentopia, "What is Biometrics?" Opentopia, http://encycl.opentopia.com/term/Biometrics (Accessed March 16, 2011).
9. Ibid.
10. IdentityTheftFixes, "Biometrics."
11. Tommy's Blog, "Mortgage Fraud Prevention with E-Signature and Digital Signatures," Quality Mortgage Services, http://www.qualitymortgageservices.com/qmsblog/qmsblog/compliance-techology/mortgage-fraud-prevention-with-e-signature-and-digital-signatures/ (Posted May 20, 2010).
12. Ibid.
13. Tina L. Douglas, "E-Signatures and Identity Theft," Ezine Articles.com, http://ezine

articles.com/?E-Signatures-and-Identity-Theft&id=4688720, (Accessed October 3, 2010).

14. Ibid.

15. Tommy's Blog, "Mortgage Fraud Prevention."

16. Search Security, "Digital Signature (Electronic Signature)," Search Security, http://searchsecurity.techtarget.com/sDefinition/0,,sid14_gci211953,00.html (Accessed March 17, 2011).

17. Douglas, "E-Signatures."

18. Douglas, "E-Signatures."

19. eHow, "How to Prevent Identity Theft and Secure Data with PGP," eHow.com, http://www.ehow.com/how_5282367_prevent-theft-secure-data-pgp.html (Accessed August 31, 2010).

20. Madison Bank, "Online Security: Encryption Methods," Bankwithmadison.com, https://www.bankwithmadison.com/online-security/ (Accessed July 19, 2011).

21. Ibid.

22. Ibid.

23. eHow, "How to Prevent Identity Theft."

24. Ibid.

25. Keith Regan, "Can Legislation Stop Identity Theft?" CRM Buyer, http://www.crmbuyer.com/story/49099.html?wlc=1287595887 (Posted March 1, 2006).

26. Ibid.

27. Ibid.

28. Ibid.

29. Ibid.

30. Ronald W. Mortensen, "Illegal, but Not Undocumented: Identity Theft, Document Fraud, and Illegal Employment," The Center for Immigration Studies, http://www.cis.org/identitytheft (Posted June 2009).

31. Ibid.

32. Steve Bates, "SHRM Sues to Block E-Verify Mandate for Contractors," Society for Human Resource Management, http://www.shrm.org/Publications/HRNews/Pages/SHRMSuesoverEVerify.aspx (Posted December 24, 2008).

33. McMillan, "Belarus Man Pleads Guilty."

34. Bates, "SHRM Sues."

35. Mortensen, "Illegal, but Not Undocumented."

36. Debbie Dujanovic, "Investigative Report: Could Your Child's ID Already Be Stolen?" KSL-TV, http://www.ksl.com/index.php?nid=148&sid=160060 (Posted February 6, 2006).

37. Mortensen, "Illegal, but Not Undocumented."

38. Mortensen, "Illegal, but Not Undocumented."

39. Aaron Emigh, "Online Identity Theft: Phishing Technology, Chokepoints and Countermeasures," Anti-Phishing Working Group, http://www.antiphishing.org/Phishing-dhs-report.pdf (Posted October 3, 2005).

CHAPTER 8

1. Jamie Frator and Erin R., "10 Bizarre Cases of Identity Theft," Listverse, http://listverse.com/2009/09/05/

10-bizarre-cases-of-identity-theft/ (Posted September 5, 2010).

2. Credit Identity Safe.com, "Esther Reed—The Secret Life of a Sophisticated Identity Thief," Credit Identity Safe, http://creditidentitysafe.com/idtheft/esther-reed.htm (Posted February 8, 2008).

3. SwinneySwitch, "Undercover Operation Cracked Illegal Alien Network," *Free Republic*, http://www.freerepublic.com/focus/f-news/1949019/posts (Posted January 4, 2008).

4. Steven Malanga, "Illegal in More Ways than One," *City Journal*, http://www.city-journal.org/2008/18_2_snd-identity_theft.html (Accessed July 19, 2011).

5. Phoenix Business Journal, "Identity Theft 911 Report Blames Illegal Immigration, Government Inaction for State's Top Ranking," *Phoenix Business Journal*, http://www.bizjournals.com/phoenix/stories/2008/03/03/daily17.html?t=printable (Posted March 4, 2008).

6. Ronald W. Mortensen, "Illegal, but Not Undocumented: Identity Theft, Document Fraud, and Illegal Employment," The Center for Immigration Studies, http://www.cis.org/identitytheft (Posted June, 2009).

7. Ibid.

8. Ibid.

9. Department of Homeland Security, "Remarks by Secretary of Homeland Security Michael Chertoff, Immigration and Customs Enforcement Assistant Secretary Julie Myers, and Federal Trade Commission Chairman Deborah Platt Majoras at a Press Conference on Operation Wagon Train," Department of Homeland Security, http://www.dhs.gov/xnews/releases/pr_1166047951514.shtm (Posted December 13, 2006).

10. Bob Sullivan, "The Secret List of ID Theft Victims: Consumers Could Be Warned, but U.S. Government Isn't Talking," MSNBC, http://www.msnbc.msn.com/id/6814673 (Posted January 29, 2005).

11. Ibid.

◯ ◯ ◯ FURTHER RESOURCES ◯ ◯ ◯

IDENTITY THEFT EDUCATION RESOURCES

Spend On Life

http://www.spendonlife.com

This Web site offers numerous articles about identity theft risks and prevention. Articles include: "Steps to Prevent Child Identity Theft," "Change of Address Identity Theft," "How to Get a Child's Credit Report," "How to Know if Your Identity Has Been Stolen," "Identity Theft Protection Guide," "Placing a Fraud Alert on Your Credit Report," and "Who Really Needs Your Social Security Number?"

FEDERAL TRADE COMMISSION RESOURCES

Items on the following list consist of identity theft reports, practical tips to help consumers minimize their risk, steps victims should take, the latest national and state trends, survey data, testimony, comments, and an overview of the FTC's Identity Theft Program.

Consumer Publications Related to Identity Theft
http://www.ftc.gov/bcp/edu/microsites/idtheft/consumers/consumer-publications.html

Data from the FTC's September 2003 Identity Theft Survey Report
http://www.ftc.gov/bcp/edu/microsites/idtheft/downloads/synovate_report.pdf

Data from the FTC's September 2006 Identity Theft Survey Report
http://www.ftc.gov/os/2007/11/SynovateFinalReportIDTheft2006.pdf

Federal Trade Commission's Identity Theft Program—Overview (October 1998–September 2003)
http://www.ftc.gov/bcp/edu/microsites/idtheft/downloads/ftc_overview_id_theft.pdf

First Steps a Victim Should Take
  http://www.ftc.gov/bcp/edu/microsites/idtheft/consumers/
  defend.html

General Consumer Information About Identity Theft
  http://www.ftc.gov/bcp/edu/microsites/idtheft/consumers/
  about-identity-theft.html

National Trends in Fraud and Identity Theft Complaints
  http://www.ftc.gov/bcp/edu/microsites/idtheft/reference-desk/
  national-data.html

State Trends in Fraud and Identity Theft Complaints
  http://www.ftc.gov/bcp/edu/microsites/idtheft/reference-desk/
  state-data.html

Test Your Knowledge About Identity Theft
  http://onguardonline.gov/media

Testimony Presented by the FTC
  http://www.ftc.gov/bcp/edu/microsites/idtheft/reference-desk/
  reports-2006-2007.html

Tips to Help Consumers Minimize Their Risk
  http://www.ftc.gov/bcp/edu/microsites/idtheft/consumers/deter.
  html

FEDERAL IDENTITY THEFT LAWS

CAN-SPAM Act of 2003
  http://www.spamlaws.com/federal/can-spam.shtml

Check 21: Check Clearing for the 21st Century Act
  http://www.fdic.gov/consumers/consumer/alerts/check21.html

FACTA: Fair and Accurate Credit Transactions Act of 2003
  http://frwebgate.access.gpo.gov/cgi-bin/getdoc.
  cgi?dbname=108_cong_public_laws&docid=f:publ159.108

FCRA: Fair Credit Reporting Act
   http://www.ftc.gov/os/statutes/031224fcra.pdf

FDCPA: Fair Debt Collection Practices Act
   http://www.ftc.gov/os/statutes/fdcpa/fdcpact.htm

Identity Theft and Assumption Deterrence Act
   http://www.ftc.gov/os/statutes/itada/itadact.htm

STATE IDENTITY THEFT LAWS

Find Law
   http://law.findlaw.com/state-laws/identity-theft/
   Select a state to read about its laws governing identity theft.

IDENTITY THEFT CASES AND SCAMS

Identity Theft Fixes
   http://www.identitytheftfixes.com/
   A Web site dedicated to "Protecting Your Identity with Every-
   thing We've Got" and offering numerous articles and resources,
   including: "Are ATMs an Increasing Identity Theft Target?,"
   "Common Identity Theft Scams," "Don't Let the Dancing Pigs
   Fool You," "Facebook Identity Theft Scams," "Medical Identity
   Theft Is On the Rise," "Online Work or Identity Theft Scams,"
   "Texting and Phishing—A Dangerous Combination," "You Didn't
   Win the Lotto: You've Been the Victim of Identity Theft."

JOHN VACCA is an information technology consultant and internationally known best-selling author based in Pomeroy, Ohio. Since 1982, John has authored 69 books. Some of his most recent books include: *System Forensics, Investigation, and Response*; *Managing Information Security*; *Network and Systems Security*; *Computer and Information Security Handbook*; *Biometric Technologies and Verification Systems*; *Practical Internet Security*; *Optical Networking Best Practices Handbook*; *Guide to Wireless Network Security*; *Computer Forensics: Computer Crime Scene Investigation, 2nd Edition*; *Firewalls: Jumpstart For Network And Systems Administrators*; *Public Key Infrastructure: Building Trusted Applications and Web Services*; and *Identity Theft*. He is also the author of more than 600 articles in the areas of advanced storage, computer security, and aerospace technology. John was also a configuration management specialist, computer specialist, and the computer security official (CSO) for NASA's space station program (Freedom) and the International Space Station Program, from 1988 until his retirement from NASA in 1995. In addition, John was one of the security consultants for the MGM movie *AntiTrust* (2001). More information can be viewed at http://www.johnvacca.com.

MARY E. VACCA worked for the aerospace industry, providing information technology (IT) support to the National Aeronautics and Space Administration's (NASA) Shuttle Program Office in Houston, Texas, for more than 20 years, until her retirement in 1995. Her work as a system engineer in developing management information systems gave her broad experience in identity management, computer security, networking, software development, and quality control. Mary was the lead system engineer for a meeting support system that combined hardware and software applications to support real-time online meetings being conducted between personnel located at the various NASA sites. She has also authored many technical documents during her career. Due to her love of writing, as an avocation, she has also coauthored three novels, one of which won second place for best novel in two writing contests. She has since spent much of her time writing short stories, poems, and nonfiction books.